I0393608

GRAFFITI VERITE' 19 (GV19)
Special 1974 Commemorative Reissue Series

IMPRESSIONS

Magazine of the Arts

Volume 1 Number 4
Original Publication: June 1976

Reissue for Educational & Historical Reference Use Only

Disclaimer:

All Promotional Advertisements, Store Addresses, Events, Telephone Numbers, Magazine Location, Product Sale Prices and Magazine Subscription information within the Original Publication issue are no longer, in most cases, in existence and/or applicable.

Please direct all inquires regarding the Special 1974 Commemorative Reissue of the GV19 IMPRESSIONS MAGAZINE (2012) to:

IMPRESSIONS MAGAZINE

c/o BRYAN WORLD PRODUCTIONS
P.O. Box 74033 Los Angeles, CA 90004 USA
website: www.graffitiverite.com
e-mail: bryworld@aol.com

(c) Copyright 1974-2012 Robert Bryan, Publisher, IMPRESSIONS Black Arts & Culture Magazine, IMPRESSIONS Magazine of the Arts, BRYAN WORLD PRODUCTIONS.
All Rights Reserved.

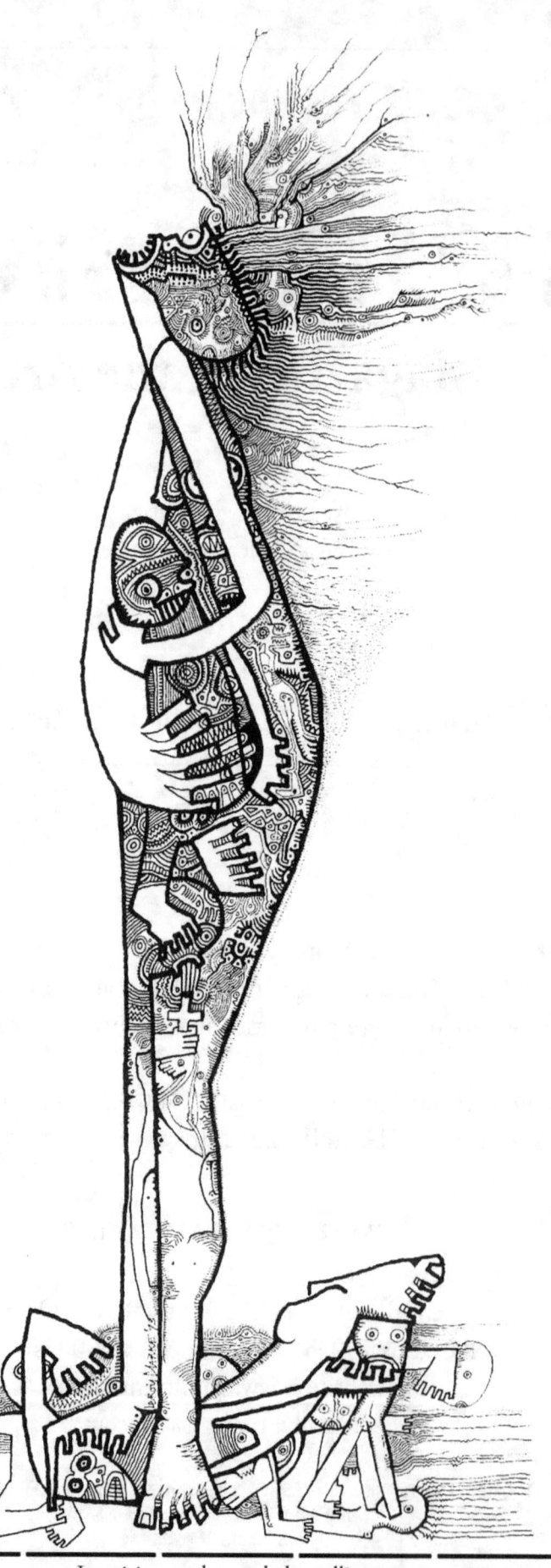

Douens... 1973 to 1975
a new series of paintings, drawings and poems.

by LeRoy Clarke

Inquiries can be made by calling or writing LeRoy Clarke at these addresses:

840 Montgomery St. Brooklyn 11213
(212) 467-6435
Clarkes 2 Hermitage Rd. Berlmont
Port of Spain Trinidad, West Indies

IMPRESSIONS

VOLUME ONE/NUMBER FOUR/JUNE 1976   MAGAZINE OF THE ARTS

contents

DEPARTMENTS

RECORD REVIEWS
8

BOOK REVIEWS
9

EXPOSURE
10

LIFELINES
40

Publisher
Robert Bryan

Editorial Director
Calvin Wilson

Contributing Editors:

Joyce Dukes
David Edwards
Hector Lino, Jr.
Jann Parker
Victor Manuel Rosa
Ntozake Shange
John A. Williams
Ernell Elizabeth Worrell

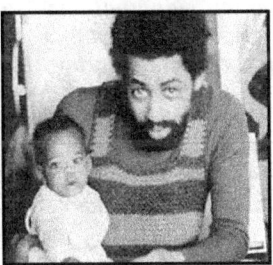

Mayya and father Bob Bryan
Photo by Pat Glenn

MUSIC

4   Jon Lucien: Journey To Enlightenment

7   Machito at Town Hall

15   Blue Magic: Philly Soul

22   Oscar Brown, Jr.: Movin' On

THEATER

16   Barbara Ann Teer and The National Black Theater

19   Excerpt from Bill Gunn's play *Black Picture Show*

34   Adrienne Kennedy: The Dream Experience On Stage

44   Point of View: Cleavon Little and Dick Anthony Williams

COVER STORY

28   Melvin Van Peebles: From *Sweetback* to *The True American*

LITERATURE

12   Piri Thomas: Down These New Roads

18   *How She Got Over:* A Short Story by Ernell Elizabeth Worrell

55   Excerpt from Melvin Van Peebles' *The True American*

ART

11   Caroline Anderson

37   The Power of Art: Dr. Ademola Talks About His Work

FILM

26   Woodie King, Jr. Directs *The Long Night*

DANCE

7   *The New Art Ensemble*

POETRY

36

Impressions Magazine, Volume 1, Number 4, June 1976 issue. © Copyright 1976 by **Impressions Magazine.** Permission to use any interviews, essays, photographs, excerpts of novels, fiction, artwork must be made in writing to **Impressions Magazine** before use. All rights reserved. Views expressed by contributors within the text of **Impressions** are   not to be construed as being the views of **Impressions Magazine.** All submitted work must include a self-addressed stamped envelope. Mailing address: **IMPRESSIONS MAGAZINE,** Lincolnton Station, Drawer Z, 2266 Fifth Avenue, New York, New York 10037. Telephone:(212) Ju 6-3700 Subscription rates: 6 issues $4.50 and 12 issues $9.00.

Jon Lucien
JOURNEY TO
ENLIGHTENMENT

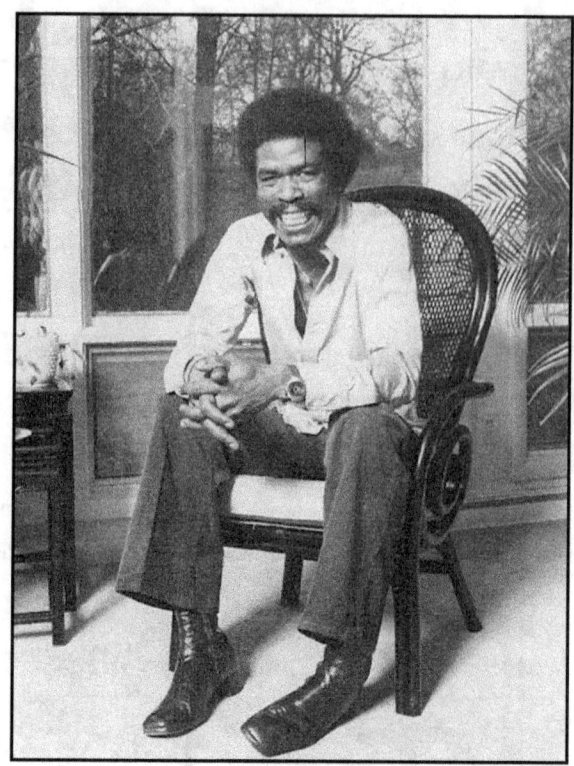

Photo Courtesy - Columbia Records

Introduction by Bob Bryan

Jon Lucien creates the kind of musical experience that easily evokes the question: "Where has he been all of our Lives?" The truth being that Lucien is a spiritual presence that has been around and within us for a long time.

Jon's New York City stage introduction occurred in 1972, at no other place than the world-famous Apollo Theater, thanks to the perceptivity of Frankie "Hollywood" Crocker. Mr. Crocker (known for having the best ear in the business), being one of the top D.J.s in the world, immediately seized upon the newly-released Dindi track by RCA in that year, giving it airplay. For New York it was a happening, for we were listening to the sensitive lyrics of Ray Gilbert:

Wind that speaks to the leaves
Telling stories that no one believes
Stories of Love belong to you and me.
With original music by Antonio Carlos Jobim, Dindi, as interpreted by Jon, took on new life and meaning.

Jon was born on Tortola, an island in the West Indies, and was taught to play bass by his blind musician father. Jon's talent as a song stylist is a gift inherited from his mother. With this rare blend of talent, Jon came to New York, eager to break into the music world.

Having paid his dues as a musician and singer, Jon has become an important new force in music, transcending categories and labels. To Jon's credit he has recorded 3 albums for RCA: I AM NOW (1970), RASHIDA (1973) and MIND'S EYE (1974). During the summer of 1975 Jon released his debut album for Columbia, SONG FOR MY LADY, which has firmly established him as a major recording star.

On the liner notes for the RASHIDA album, Henry Mancini wrote, "Very rarely does an album appear on the scene that takes a listener and transforms him into a viewer. RASHIDA does just that . . .and it's exciting." Subsequently two songs from that album, the title track RASHIDA and LADY LOVE, won Grammy nominations for best arrangement accompanying a vocalist.

Writing the Majority of the music which he records, Jon publishes his music under his own Ke-Bo Music Corp. and continues, in my estimation, to pen some of the best lyrics in the business.

Jon's music is his message and if you haven't dug it, I strongly recommemd that you do not hesitate to pick up on this unique musical experience.

Jon strongly impresses me as a man of the earth, totally relaxed in his element and at home wherever he is. Impressions is delighted to introduce to all of our readers a star in every sense of the word, and a very nice man, Jon Lucien. Enjoy.

Bob Bryan: What kind of reponse have you been receiving to the kind of music that you've been recording?

Jon Lucien: Well. . .I'm flattered, because for a long time I've been trying to be me, be myself, and the more I've been being myself, the more difficult things became. Everybody was telling me, "No, man, you got to do this, you got to do that", and I'm feelin' inside, "No, I don't gotta do that, I don't gotta do it, man". . .and I starve a little bit longer. I ain't going to do it (laugh), and it was a rough struggle, but now that I left. . .I wouldn't completely put RCA down, 'cause at least it gave me a chance to keep doin' things, keep making records, but they didn't expose me, y'know.

Bob: They didn't give you the publicity that you needed?

Jon: No, they didn't do nothin' like that. They just put the record out, give me a little token here, token there, and blah, blah, blah. I mean, I live in New York, so I have no way of knowing what's going on in the other cities (laugh). But after going with CBS and making a tour for the first time to these other cities. . .in some cities, they think that MIND'S EYE was my first album. Some people thought that RASHIDA was the first. Some thought that RASHIDA was my second. Some think that I AM NOW is the third, because the whole thing is just mixed up. Because suddenly, from the CBS promotion, they dig everything up.

Bob: How do you relate to your music being put in a category?

Jon: I didn't understand what they meant. . .a category? I don't have a category. Music is not a category. But in this country everything is categorized. For a West Indian person, they expect you only to play Caribbean music. If you're black they expect only R&B or Blues. . .you're not supposed to be able to do anything other than that so-called ethnic background

Bob: When you look at the albums that you've done for RCA, including the ones now that you've done for Columbia, how would you talk about your musical evolution up to now?

Jon: I try to express a growth every time I appear in a record. I definitely see the growth from the I AM NOW to SONG FOR MY LADY albums.

Bob: In what way do you see the growth?

Jon: Well, musically I've developed. Vocally I've developed. My voice is more subtle than on the I AM NOW album. I've gained more confidence in recording studios; I have more of an understanding from the production end of the thing because. . .fortunately for me, I write my own music and I create

everything from scratch. So when I go into the studio and put it down, I know where everything is going. Except when it comes to the horns and the strings, which I don't write, but I get together with an arranger and we discuss how and why. . .so that gives me a deeper insight as to the overall product of record-making. Then I start to view what was commercial and what wasn't commercial and try to make certain that I didn't get caught up into trying to be a commercial artist, but whatever I do comes from a natural essence, rather than sitting there and trying to create this bag or trying to create that for these people. Like now, on CBS they want a single. Now, I have no objections to singles, 'cause they feel that they can put me over with a single. But the single has to be something that Jon Lucien identifies with, that relates to Jon Lucien; no matter what it is.

David Edwards: Instead of covering somebody's record.

Jon: Yeah, right. So what happens now is that I went home and without even thinking about it I wrote a song, and it comes out IF I COULD. I've never even tried to write a song, but this particular day I was just playing and I was thinking about the Jazz Crusaders, and they have a thing about them that puts you right into that thing, y'know (group laughter). So I was just messing with this piano, and I came up with this groove and it expresses me; it expresses the kinds of things that I say lyrically. /but you can definitely see that it is the most commercial thing that has come out of me. So I kind of look at it as maybe. . .this might be what they can relate to, where they can say yeah, this is more commerical. 'Cause I could hear it and relate to certain things that I am hearing in the street, that it is commercial. The moment I played it to them. . .I thought maybe they were going to want a Thom Bell or something like that. . .so I just sat there. I had a tape recording of myself at the piano and accompaniment and I sat there. Suddenly their feet. . .they started tappin'. . .the feet of the big guys. I was just holding it, y'know. When the tape was finished the guy jumped up from behind his desk and applauded. He said, "Jon, this is the single!" So I said, "Well I'm happy that you say that because this is what I thought you all might have been looking for. Although I didn't stop and intentionally try to do this; it just came out this way."

David: All things must pass.

Jon: So maybe it's a Buddhist thing, cause and effect. Maybe it's like, Jon, OK, you do this, but still I have the rest of my work. My work is still developing. I got a waltz that is so Africano (laugh),

it is so black. . .I just sit up and listen. When you listen to my new record, and my percussionist (Ralph McDonald) playing with me, you hear a lot of (creates sounds of drums) and I'm reciting a poem. There are no words until the poem comes, but I'm singing without the words. . .multiple voices until the poem, and I recite the poem. But in the song *Journey To Enlightenment* I relate to the mystic laws of cause and effect.

David: I was going to ask you about that.

Jon: So I didn't say Nam Myoho Renge Kyo, but I spoke about cause and effect and tuning yourself up to the universe, and I did the old song, *Laura*. I wrote a couple of other things and I introduced Phyllis Hyman. She's working up at Rust Brown's and when I saw her she blew my mind. She's singing a duet with me on a song called *Spring's Arrival*.

David: This is on your new album?

Bob: When is that scheduled to be released?

Jon: Yeah. It's finished. They just have to come up with a cover. Because we're actually finished. What blew their mind is that we went into the studios, pop, pop, pop, pop, and it was done.

Bob: You mentioned Buddhism, the way to enlightenment. Could you tell us how you happened to have gotten involved with that, and describe the basic teachings?

Jon: Well, mainly, it does not segregate, y'know. I was a Christian Catholic, went to Catholic school and everything. And like I could not understand the Father, the Son and the Holy Ghost. So I would say to the father, "Bless me father for I have sinned," and I'd tell him all about the cookies that I stole, pennies. . .silly stuff. And He's supposed to be cleaning my sins away, and there is no such thing. How could this man like me wash my sins away and I see him uptown at the apothecary drinking liquor, and he's washing my sins. . . and he doesn't have on his robes anymore, he took the robe off so he can go uptown and. . .I mean how is this guy gonna tell me? I'm looking at these statues in the church, and there are all these saints and everbody, and they're all white. Nobody's relating to me. There was no relationship, no good connection. So I quit the Catholic school and went to public school, and what I did was just try to relate to the things that I saw that were most natural around me. I mean, the way the animals were living, the plants, how they were growing. I always had a piece of ground. I used to plant red beans and cabbage and everything. And I could see by watering these seeds that they would grow. So I started to dig what was hap-

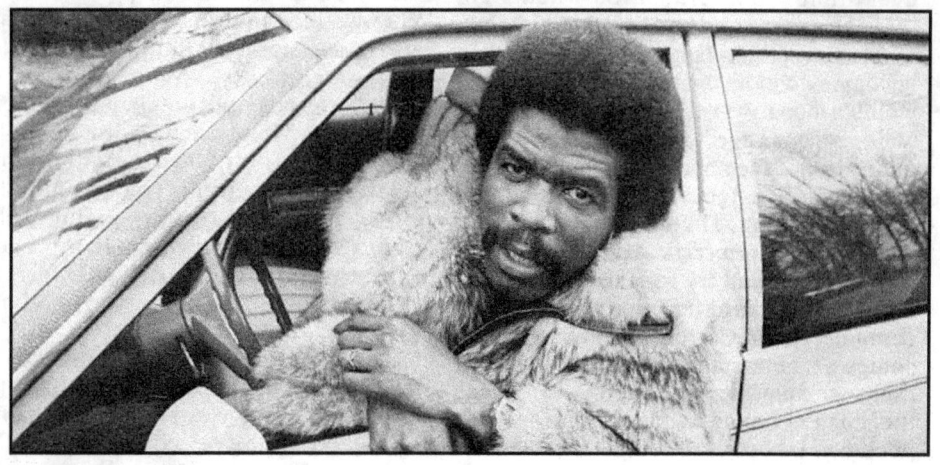

pening naturally, the fruits, what they were good for, what they did, the different plants, the different teas, what they were for, etc. And I would read everything that had to do with the spiritual being. Instead of being in some church and playing blah, blah, blah and when you walk out of church, you're full of it again. That didn't make no sense to me; so this July it'll be two years that I've been practicing Nam Myoho Renge Kyo. It was introduced to me and explained that Nam Myoho Renge Kyo is the devotion of the mind and the body to the laws of cause and effect through sound. I said "whaaaat" (laughter) and I said, "well how do you do this?"... Actually when you are chanting, the vibrations buzz through you body and you begin to realize that you've got the knowledge inside you. Knowledge that you did not know existed, and that you cannot get by reading books. The books are an exercise, a mental and verbal exercise. I discovered that you go through college and never find that peace and that enlightenment within yourself. You can never tune up to the universe outside your being, which is all the space around us.

Bob: What is the connection between sound and enlightenment?

Jon: Well, it's like a vibration. If, for instance, you're sick and you're hurting and you want some help, if you don't make a sound, some kind of a shout or something, there's not going to be any connection. If you don't take the hammer and hit the nail, the nail ain't going to go inside the wood. So when you chant (begins to chant), like all over your body you feel it, the thing just goes zzzzzzzzz all through you, and at the same time the universe is hearing you, but if you go (goes silent) and you're meditating in silence and you get up and you start giving flowers to people, walking around in white robe on "you're so saintful"... This is today, you need money to survive, you do a gig...in

Buddhism you've got to work. Buddhism is unity; we all become a family. We help each other. I help you to get your practice together with what you don't know in the practice. What I don't know in the practice, you help me. We come together, we do the practice together. It's all based on...if you want to better yourself, you must apply yourself to the practice, 'cause you're not doing anybody no favor by doing it. You don't have to do anything that you don't want to do. But the only reason that I turn people on to this is because I saw actual proof. When I started to do my practice, I was playing at the Top of the Gate that weekend. I didn't know where the next gig was coming from, just happy that people were coming down there. And Lugoff kept saying, yeah, come on back next weekend. So we kept going back and suddenly right after that gig was over, just before it was over, some dude came down to the Gate and said that this guy (referring to himself) has got to be presented like he is on his album, and that was a man named DON FRIEDMAN. And I had just started to chant...just started doing it! The next thing I knew, I was in Philharmonic Hall with this orchestra with these strings, with voices (laughter). Suddenly it was a complete BOOM...changed. And as of that point everyting started to change and grow and grow and grow and I started to get a following and I said, "Well, how do they know about me (referring to his audience)?

David: They knew you all the time.

Jon: They knew me all the time, just by this person turning that person on and this person turning this person on, b ab ab b ab ab ab a. And the place was filled, standing room only. It blew my mind and when I came out the people went (Roarrrr)...my knees buckled because it was the first time that I had really ever been any place headlining.

Bob: Was there anybody in your life by the name of Rashida?

Jon: No, but there was a person, an

actual person. It's just that I didn't use that name. "Rashida" was more musical, and when you write I don't think the your personal life should be that completely exposed (laughter). You can tell by some of my songs that they are my actual experiences. I don't know how I learnt to write the words in the way I use them and say things in the way I do. It just comes, that's just the way I say it. It's most natural for me, and it's musical. A poet can give me a beautiful poem, but it may not be musical because of the types of words that he's using; they're too hard, or they're more for speaking than for being melodious. Speaking of love is a thing that I craved for, maybe because I've been away from my family for so young. When I was a kid, I was 9 years old, I went into a school for boys who had problems. Those are the kind of schools that they call reformatory schools. I wasn't a crook or anything...I just played hooky (laughter). I couldn't be with those nuns. I wanted to play music and play ball.

David: Where was this?

Jon: In St. Thomas, in the islands.

Bob: I kow that your father was blind and that he taught you how to play... would you say that your father's inspiration has anything to do with the emotional colors that are painted by your music?

Jon: I can't say no and I can't say yes because it came through him...our musical ability came through my father. He's always been a musician, he still is a musician and all of us came out touched with a musical ability. Now when I left home, I knew a couple of chords that he had shown me, and I went to this school and I messed with them same chords, and then I became a bass player with him, and that's when my imagination started to spread further. Then I hooked up with a guy from England and I started to play Jazz and my mind started to go somewhere else altogether. It was another place, and I said WOW. All of these influences affected my growth; the music just took over. In school, when I was supposed to be doing math, I was (beating drums). I'm hearing (points to his head) some stuff, I'm trying to work it out, y'know. I'm working it out on the desk, when I'm supposed to be doing the math. (laughter) So the basic thing started from my father...on my mother's side everybody sings, which is a mind-blower (laugh). I mean, little kids...I went up to Tortola to visit my folks, and the little kids are sitting on the steps, and before they went to go to bed they decided to sing some tunes, and tears just dropped from my eyes because they

Cont'd on page 60

Otis Sallid

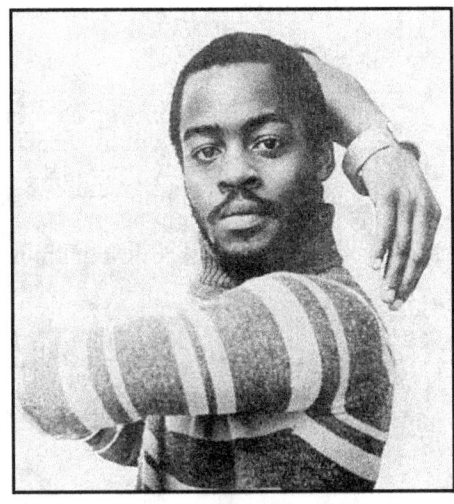

"I was born to be a dancer, choreographer, in the theatre. At this moment, I'm doing it. I never had any doubts about what I was supposed to be. And since I was four years old, I knew that I would choreograph, and then go on to be a director, and then go on to be a producer, and then deal with film."

-Otis Sallid

February 8, 1976, at the Harlem Performance Center, deserves a special kind of celebration. Good experiences are like that, making you feel and respond non-verbally like a scat or rift, or crazy staccato-like vibrations. The rush is uncontrollable as you lean forward in your seat for a better view. The exclaimation is, WOW!

The New Art Ensemble are a group of expressionist weavers of a complete dimension; sight, sound, touch and taste. The medium is dance; a strange mixture of leaps, springs, steps, and falls which announce the entrance of another's vision into our lives. The dancers and the choreographer see and feel, and they let us know that. They author a sensual/social excursion that turns romance into a stage play to be felt, understood, and hopefully seen a little more clearly.

The vignettes are very urban in texture. The movements are frenzied yet clear, balletic yet black, modern yet Harlem funk. We are witnesses to the

By Hector Lino, Jr.

confusion in human relationshi ps. We are visited by the blues and the dull greens of people trying to understand each other; the angry reds and impassioned pinks of unrequited love; and the ethos of the urban Black experience, that slips through our defenses and colors our relationships with people we love.

The New Art Ensemble manages to avoid the weird mechanics and computerized choreography of the 70's. The dance is cinematic in texture. The pieces move like well-paced scenes in a good film, allowing the mood and the statements to connect and give a wholesomeness to the message. *The New Art Ensemble gives you new variations on the old song.*

For Otis Sallid, the choreographer for the group and the director of Place and Visions Dance Studio, dance is much more than an entertainment vehicle. It's a locality for human expression and spiritual exploration. Says Otis, "Dance, music, drama are all the same in the sense that they allow people to see things they haven't seen before and to become educated to new experiences."

Otis uses choreography much like an abstract painter. The images are both bizarre and beautiful. He doesn't flavor his work with the "right" way of doing things. Sallid is much more interested in whether or not he is able to stimulate a response and create an experience for the audience. "I break all the rules and I discover new rules to be broken; nothing is really new, it's just the use of space and time that is. I do very anti-climatic things; some pieces end wrong, but you have to be daring and ignore conventions if you want to affect people.

The motivation behind Sallid's experiments is to find the center and bridge the gap between the major dance schools—Ballet, Modern, Jazz, African, East Indian, etc.—and to create a new dance form, one that allows for the freedom of all and eliminates their limitations. The new form Sallid is searching for will expand the reach of the artist

Cont'd on page 53

MACHITO
At Town Hall

It could have been 1943 at the Broadway Palladium: *Babarabatiri* sounded that exhiliratingly recent. Macho (the nickname MC Stella Marrs, "Lady Disc jockey for WRVR-FM", called this real STAR by) exhibited a showmanship and stage charisma garnered from thousands of performances from Rio de *Janeiro* to Panama City to Madrid. Here was the leader of "The World's Greatest Latin Dance Band": Machito & his Afro-Cubans playing to a half-filled Town Hall. And the occasion was no less exalted by this concert being the CBA (Collective Black Artist) salute to the world famous vocalist/maraquero and the presence of its ensemble, which on this evening included alto and tenor saxists, respectfully, Justo Almario and Bill Saxon, former frontline hornmen of the Mongo Santamaria group. Both thoroughly grounded in the school of Hard Bop and at home with the polyrhythmics of Black Hispanic Music, their solos burned inside melodies riffing off Nilo Serra's bass, Mike Rios' piano, Papo Pepin', conga and Mario Grill's (Machito's son) timbales, often with delicious rhythm inventions embellished by the CBA ensemble's startlingly lucid and becoming passages. No forced hybrids here; here was a natural cultural confluence of Third World Americana: a "fusion of Latin and Jazz" that would fill the hearts of Luciano "Chano" Pozo and Charlie "Bird" Parker with glee upon seeing the continuation of their former colleagues' fervourous dedication to the pursuit of this conjugal music.

Featured on this evening was Chico O'Farrill, the arranging/composing genius who integrated Bird's sophisticated alto harmonies with Jose Mangual's complex conga drumming in the early 50's (*Soul Source*, Verve). Nearly 25 years later, O'Farrill did the same with Gato Barbieri's lyrical legato wail and Luis Mangual/Ray Armando/Ray Mantilla/Portinho's more than just "latin percussion". In the interim, he headed big bands in Cuba and Mexico and worked with Dizzy Gillespie, Miguelito Valdes, Art Farmer, Count Basie and Clark Terry among others, O'Farrill expertly conducted the last movement of his classic *Afro-Cuba Jazz Suit* (originally written for Machito, it appeared on their aforementioned Verve LP).

As alluded to before, Bird masterfully soloed on the original; this time it was Sonny Fortune, with his trusty alto saxophone, who potently improvised within diasporial folk contexts not specifically his own. Of course, with a vocabulary enriched by Ornette Coleman's, Eric Dolphy's and John Coltrane's (recent key pioneers of contemporary saxophone playing) these contributions made his instrument's commentary distinct from that of the late BeBop great but still reminiscent of the latter's intense sonic beauty.

Other highlights of the evening were the CBA ensemble's fine, nostalgic rendering of *Mambo Inn* and *Cuban Fantasy*. Mambo Era standards whose precise execution, with the aid of Kenny Rogers' growling baritone saxophone, lent the pieces a timelessness that must have conjured up for older aficionados images of these masters as young experimenters, perhaps at the defunct Blackhawk in San Francisco or, even earlier, at La Conga here in NYC.

Not that youth wasn't represented among these distinguished elders; there were the young and capable Angel Fernanadez (in his late teens) and Clifford Adams (middle twenties) in the trumpet and trombone sections, respectfully. And who can forget John Faddis' Gillespian trumpet fluency on *Afro-Cuban Jazz Suite*, a stellar performance displaying virtuosic ability beyond his tender years. Sitting beside them was Charlie Persip, veteran of Afro-Cuban Bop aggregations of the past, who recently has been trap drumming with Archie Shepp, adding to the magic.

Throughout it all, seeing Machito in action was a delight, with his slightly undulating hips, arms up in the air tracing his dance steps, gesturing with microphone in hand for orchestral leaps and bounds from Almario/Saxon/Rogers/Persip and company. His is a sonero's voice, strong and well-seasoned in the certainty of its generic experience, no longer just telling Havana-New York stories but Intra-Hemispheric tales; caressing and tantalizing the audience with, for example, *Buscando La Melodia*(Looking for the Melody). No matter that the setting was specifically Bahia/Black Brazil during Carnaval; the quest of New World griots from Bahia to Chicago was captured in its words. As Fats Navarro, the now departed Afro-Cuban who was one of the finest trumpeters in the history of jazz, searched for a "perfect melody", being lead to marvelous streams of beauty, so it is with Machito in his seeking for a demotic melody/the song of the people. And for those of you who missed this historic affair at Town Hall, it was your very great loss. ✿

Victor Manuel Rosa

MUSIC REVIEWS

JOHN COLTRANE
THE GENTLE SIDE OF
JOHN COLTRANE
(Impulse ASH-9306-2)

These two discs showcase Coltrane's lyricism . Besides being one of the best innovators in the history of Afro-American Improvisationa; Music, he is one of its finest interpreters of ballads. Featured on these dates with him are the velvet vocals of Johnny Hartman; the late phenomenal reedman Eric Dolphy; and Duke Ellington, whose coupling with Coltrane was one of two giants. On most of the tracks Coltrane's legendary quartet (McCoy Tyner/piano, Jimmy Garrison/bass, Elvin Jones/drums, and Coltrane) works out. This collection of vintage 'Trane should not be missed.

Victor Manuel Rosa

BLUE MAGIC
THIRTEEN BLUE MAGIC LANE
(Atco SD36-120)

Magical sensuality pulsates and breathes forth from this dynamic album. Blue Magic still retains that certain flavor that brings out that style know as sensual soul.

Starring in this album is the hot single **What's Come Over Me** by Blue Magic and Margie Joseph. Ms. Joseph's voice sails as she sings strongly and sweetly about the captivating power of love.

John A. Williams

BOBBY BLAND
GET ON DOWN WITH BOBBY BLAND
(ABCD-895)

Bobby Bland is still a premier bluesman, of the Chicago Urban Electric variety, as the guitar/harmonic pickin' and riffin', in and out of a mostly pop context signifies, which at times is hampered by string arrangements. But Bobby's slightly burred voice is hautingly experiential, touching something indefinable in one. The compositions prove to be no obstacle.

V.M.R.

CECIL TAYLOR
NEFERTITI, THE BEAUTIFUL ONE HAS COME
(Arista/Freedom AL 1905)

Cecil Taylor is one of the pioneers, along with Ornette Coleman and Sun Ra, of the New Black Music (post-'60's jazz). His dazzling combination of infinite breadth of vision, virtuosic technique and relentless surrealistic

swing enriches the great legacy of Art Tatum, Thelonious Monk, Bud Powell, etc. This double LP set is no different from his other work: superlative. This is the 1963 live recording at Cafe Monmarte at Copenhagen, Denmark. Drummer Sonny Murray & Alto saxist Jimmy Lyons, both extraordinary musicians with an uncanny empathy for Taylor's music, accompany this incredible pianist.

V.M.R.

CAMILLE YARBROUGH
THE IRON POT COOKER
(Vanguard VSD 79356)

Camille Yarbrough is a poet/actress/songstress whose new album displays all of her talents superbly. She is deftly accompanied by James Benjamin, bass; Cornell Dupree, guitar; Leopoldo Fleming, congas and percussion; Jimmy Johnson, drums and percussion; Linda Twine, clavinet. DREAM-PANIC-SONNY BOY THE RIP-OFF MAN-LITTLE SALLY THE SUPER SEX STAR (TAKING CARE OF BUSINESS) is her **tour de force** collage of Black lives in progress.

V.M.R.

MARION BROWN—WITH ELLIOT SCHWARTZ & LEO SMITH
DUETS
(Arista/Freedom AL 1904)

Marion Brown is a gifted saxophonist whose love affair with Third World Music (esp. that of percussion) has taken him from jam sessions with Sengalese drummer Abraham Kobena Adzenyah to an Atlanta recording with Chicago trap drummer Steve McCall. This double LP set is a series of duets with AACM (Association for the Advancement of Colored Musicians) and Associated Trumpeter Leo Smith and Avante Garde Classical musician Elliot Schwartz. The Brown/Smith sessions are concerned with texture and color, with musicians accompanying themselves on percussion. The Brown/Schwartz sections are an exchange of Schwartz's miscellaneous invention and Brown's dry lyrical passages. These are tapes full of imagination and technique.

V.M.R.

THE REFLECTIONS
LOVE ON DELIVERY
(Capitol ST-11460)

This album contain ALL DAY, ALL NIGHT and ONE INTO ONE, songs that have gotten steady airplay, and deservedly so. The tight harmonics and strong lead vocals are noteworthy. They formerly backed Melba Moore (who wrote the liner notes). This debut album is one that exposes the talents of a group to keep an eye out for in the future.

V.M.R.

REDD FOXX
YOU GOTTA WASH YOUR ASS
(Atlantic SD-18157)

The twelve years since his last release and his subsequent elevation to a star have not affected the earthy humor belonging to the one and only Mr. Redd Foxx.

Foxx, working under the handicap of a hoarse throat, still maintains that quality that is Redd Foxx.

"You Gotta Wash Your Ass" is a Funny Album.

J.A.W.

ANTHONY BRAXTON
FIVE PIECES 1975
(Arista AL 4064)

"The Organization Man", as critic Roger Riggins has called Anthony Braxton because of his often intriguing use of "the idea of organization as a process in and of itself" in collective improvisation, is back again. His saxophone/clarinets' erudite but entertaining prose swirls around the sturdy rhythm section of Dave Holland's bass and Barry Altschul's drums, joined by trumpeter Kenny Wheeler's clear, spacious flights. Their rendition of the old standard YOU STEPPED OUT OF A DREAM is strangely reminiscent of the old Charlie Parker/Red Rodney sides.

V.M.R.

THE JIMMY CASTOR BUNCH
FEATURING THE EVERTHING MAN
"SUPERSOUND"
(Atlantic SD-18150)

The multitalented Jimmy Castor is not called "The everything man" for nothing—there are reasons. He does pratically everything musically in his album, including soprano saxophone, timbales and all background and lead vocals. This new release, "Super-sound", features the hit smash single **King Kong Part One**, which is the latest of Jimmy Castor's novelty records. This is a diversified and satisfying album that shows unique talent. My favorite when I want to cool out is called **Drifting**.

J.A.W.

RANDY WESTON
BLUES TO AFRICA
(Arista Freedom AL 1014)

These are lovely & boppish piano ruminations by Randy Weston. He has moved far enough away from his Thelonious Monk roots to find an eloquent use of time and space; to create lines that swing around melodies that have a captivating folk quality. Case in point: *African Village/Bedford Stuyvesant,* a barrel-house funk excursion into a Pan-African ethos. This is Randy Weston's first solo album and one he sould be proud of.

V.M.R.

THE IMAGINATIONS
GOOD STUFF
(20th Century T-497)

Good Stuff is not all good stuff, but enough of it is so that one can party to it without any irregularity. At itmes this disco band steps out into interesting brass/bass/voice interchange, as in MONA and YOU ARE THE LOVE OF MY LIFE, but they usually lay back, or worse meander. I think they must be aficionados of Curtis Mayfield or the Ohio Players, (who they should speak to, because it would help). I hear possibilities.

V.M.R.

TED CURSON
TEARS FOR DOLPHY
(Arista/Freedom AL 1020)

Ted Curson is an alumnus of, among others, the Charles Mingus, Cecil Taylor, and Archie Shepp aggregations. He has been living in Europe a number of years, taking the sames road many Black musicians, unable to earn a livelihood at home, have taken. An accomplished trumpeter, he has a warm, full tone & the rhythmic/harmonic dexterity of a master. He shines on the title track **Tears For Dolphy**, a brass/reed threnody in which his plaintive love cry is embellished by Bill Barron's smooth, reverent soloing on tenor. The rest of the quartet consists of Herb Bushler on bass and Dick Berk on drums.

Victor Manuel Rosa is a freelance writer.

SISTER SLEDGE
CIRCLE OF LOVE
(Atco SD36-105)

Grandma Viola Williams certainly had the right idea when she told her four grandaughters knows as Sister Sledge that they have the right edge as a singing group. Sister Sledge's recent release **Circle of Love** has shown that the right combination of talent, production, arrangement and personnel can produce a definite "yes".

John A. Williams is a freelance writer.

BOOK REVIEWS

All About Health and Beauty for the Black Woman
by Naomi Sims
(Doubleday, $8.95)

The title of this book is not an understatement, because it includes all pertinent information on the care of the entire body, from coif to pedicure. Any sister who is concerned about her basic physical appearance can benefit from its contents. **All About Health and Beauty for the Black Woman** serves as an encyclopedia to those who are not aware of the many aspects involved in keeping the body beautiful externally and internally, as well as a reference book to the informed.

Ms. Sims reaches for the nucleus of every subject dealing with the care of the body, and includes a detailed outline at the end of each chapter on the area discussed. She utilizes the knowledge of some of the country's top scientists and physicians to authenticate her observations. Skin care, for example is explained quite fully beginning with the physical properties of Black skin in accord with scientific data, following with the similarities of our skin to that of Caucasians, and finally giving exclusive attention to the basic skin types, with emphasis placed on the importance of following a specific regimen for best results.

The invisible body is given equal time, with chapters devoted to proper nutrition, posture and exercise, as well as the effects of alcohol, smoking and drugs on the external you. There are pictorial illustrations of the reproductive system and the correct procedure to be followed for self-administered breast examination. All vaginal diseases are covered and the importance of annual physical check-ups is stressed.

We are treated with bonus information in the chapters on mental health, beauty and behavior, and fashion, and a listing of hospitals and health agencies to which one can write for books and other available data on the identification and prevention of key illnesses.

Finally, I recommend this book to Black women of all ages who consider themselves special. Without a doubt, Naomi Sims has contributed a much needed book to the literary world and the Black woman, regardless of social or economic background. This one is a must.

Jann Parker is a freelance fashion writer.

Black-Eyed Susans: Classic Stories By and About Black Women
edited by Mary Helen Washington
(Anchor Books/Doubleday, $2.95)

In her introduction to this very intriguing anthology, Ms. Washington states: "It is absolutely necessary that they (black women writers) be permitted to discover and interpret the entire range and spectrum of the experiences of black women and not be stymied by preconceived conclusions." Yet the very title of the book demands that we as black woman writers view these stores as "classic", which is not the notion Alice Walker intended in her definition of a black-eyed susan: "A slight, pretty flower that grows on any ground; and flowers pledge no allegiance to banners of any man". Thus, Ms. Washington begins all over again the process which she bemoans, by grouping the finely wrought and driven stories of Jean Wheeler Smith, Toni Morrison, Gwendolyn Brooks, Louise Merriweather, Toni Cade Bambara, Alice Walker, and Paule Marshall as the 'classics' of our era. With only references made to Ann Petry, Zora Neale Hurston, Jessie Fauset, Margeret Walker, and June Jordan, I simply cannot accept this anthology as indicative of the breadth of black women writing in the United States in this century.

Further, younger, and ofter more difficult, writers are not even mentioned. Here I am thinking of Pat Parker, Alexis DeVeaux, Thulani Nkabinde, Ayida Tengemana, Ifa Iyaoun, Calua Dundy, and myriad others who have, in fact, attempted to tackle the realities of women (in Ms. Washington's words) "[who] have nervous breakdowns... are overwhelmed by sex; wives who are not faithful; women experiencing the pain and humiliation of divorce..."

The stories we are allowed by Ms. Washington do, indeed, ring with lyric and deadly actual visions of our lives as black women, and we should read them, all of them. But we mustn't be misled by the narrowness of Ms. Washington's collection. There is so much more already available. And here iks a note for publishers and seekers of women's material. A number of black women writers, with whom I have spoken about the misrepresentation of ourselves in literature have acknowledged repeated rejection of manuscripts that veer off from the loaded and pernicious perspective of black women as "the mules of the world". These women have resorted to the use of women's presses and quarterlies to publish their work.

If you are not satisfied with the scope of Ms. Washington's collection, (though each story is bold and marked with the taste/fire of the author), please, do look for the rest of black women writers whose work is not yet 'classic', but merely reaching for the truths of ourselves.

Ntozake Shange

Islands of My Mind: Poems
Habib Tiwoni
(Casha Publications, $3.00)

A mingling of black Caribbean and American sentiments, carried in a linear, sometimes 'jump-up' cadence. Tiwoni is after the truth of himself. Those of us who know what he knows, or are looking for something more of ourselves that we don't yet know, may find it here. Maybe.

Ntozake Shange

Another Voice: Feminist Perspectives on Social Life and Social Science
edited by Marcia Millman & Rosabeth Kanter
(Anchor Books Doubleday, $3.95)

A provocative and scholarly collection of sociological explorations of women's roles and possibilities in the creation/reality of the world as we know it. Yet, the fact of the denial of the significance of women in the development of our civilization, and sometimes as co-victims of our cultural pathologies, makes most of the essays assembled here virtually leap into unresearched and vast areas of our existence. There is no known equivalent of the essays; included are Gaye Tuchman's, "Women & The Creation of Culture", Lyn H. Lofland's, "The 'Thereness of Women', and Arlie Russel Hochschild's, "The Sociology of Feeling and Emotion". The phenomenon of serious feminist research and interpretation of human events is one of the more exciting episodes of our time, and Millman and Kanter have accomplished a rewarding and meticulous anthology that will surely incite more women to bring our scholarly skills and consciousness to bear on contemporary American sociology.

N.S.

Ntozake Shange is a poet and playwright, who lives in NYC. Her play For Colored Girls Who Have Considered Suicide/When The Rainbow Is Enuff *was recently produced at the New Federal Theatre.*

EXPOSURE

CONGRATULATIONS TO THE SPINNERS ON THEIR 20TH ANNIVERSARY

The Pride of New York

With a keen sense of business organization and an acute understanding of the needs of the public, the Pride of New York (a division of Spectre One, a holding company) has, in less than a year, established itself as a viable production company. Based upon the philosophy that a collective of specialists in various areas can form a powerful unit, the Pride of New York is now involved in promotion and management. The organization channels its energies into the fields of entertainment (including party planning), fine arts and fashion (it has its own staff of models and designers).

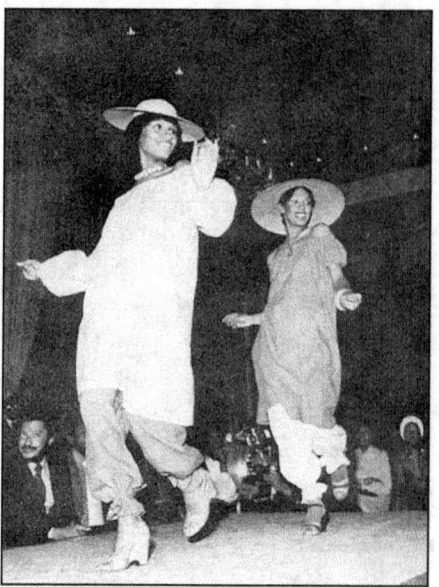

Beverly Parker, left, and Sherri "Peaches" Brewer in the Pride of New York's fashion show, at the Waldorf-Astoria.

President Raymond T. McConnell, who has been with the organization since its inception during his high school days, attributes the success of the Pride of New York to the ability of its executive board to utilize innovative business techniques, remain on top of current trends, and maintain a steady forward thrust. In affirming the commitment of the organization to "provide people with products that they need and can use," McConnell elaborates: "Black people are now consumers. In order to further advance ourselves, we must become producers."

Among the activities of the Pride of New York is the assembly of concert packages, counseling and guidance

10

programs for businesses and church groups (to help them raise money), and a travel division that organizes tour groups.

Interested groups and individuals may contact The Pride of New York at Post Office Box 1528, Wall Street Station, New York, New York 10005, (212) 247-5360.

Impact

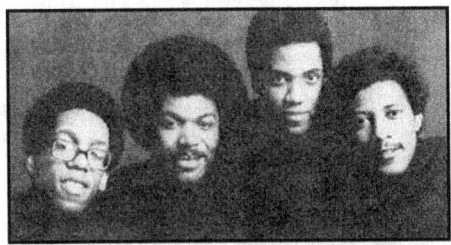

L to R: Donald Tighman, John Simms, Damon Harris, Charles Timmons.

"I got love in the palm of my hand, I'm a happy man," are the words to Damon Harris' (former lead singer of the *Temptations*) new single *Happy Man*. His new group *Impact* on ATCO Records is a sure fire hit. Producer/ Composer Bobby Eli has done it again with *Hapy Man*.

Watch out for the release of *Impact's* debut album in May!

Black Time

Black Time, a new cable television series, is produced by SR Associates in cooperation with Cell Block Theatre, Inc. (CBTV) and the Black Theatre Alliance to introduce new creative talent and showcase local business sponsorship. The series will highlight various forms of dance, poetry, and music that otherwise would have little opportunity for such broad media exposure.

Black Time is aired on Manhattan Cable Television Channel 'J' weekly, on Sundays, from 8pm-9pm.

For further information, contact Stuart Reid at SR Associates, 164 West 83rd Street, New York, New York, 10023 (212) 362-6163.

Express Yourself

in

IMPRESSIONS

For address see page 3.

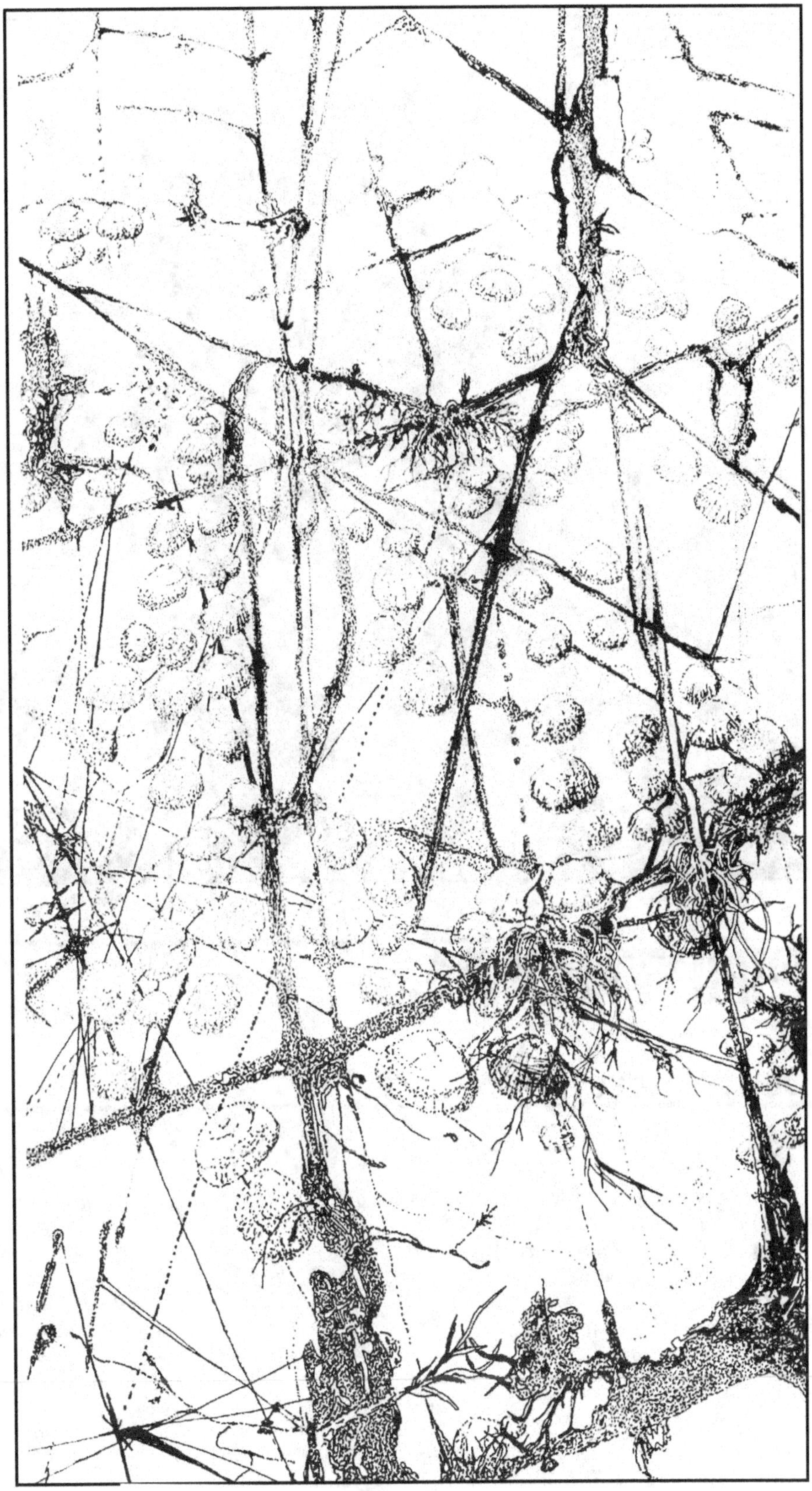

"*Self-satisfaction is the key to success. Faith in yourself enables you to reach a higher plateau.*
"*In Art the hand can never accomplish anything greater than the soul can inspire.*"

Caroline Anderson

..

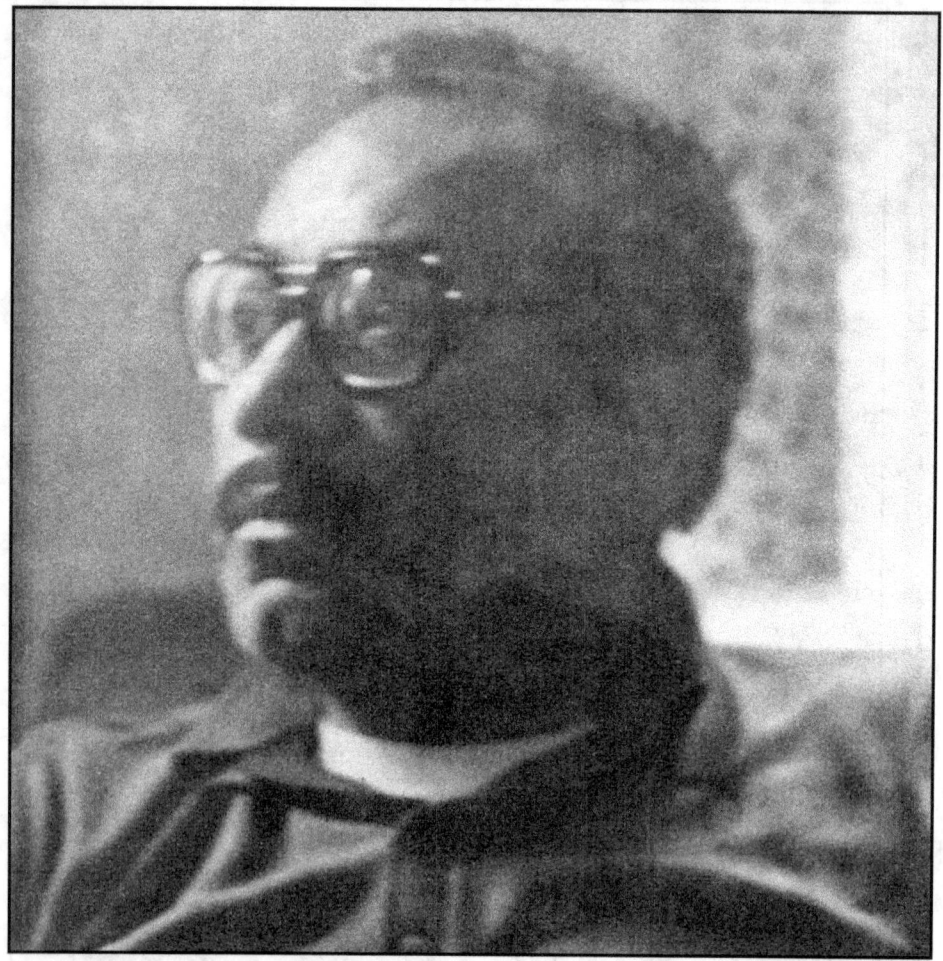

Photos by Calvin Wilson

PIRI THOMAS

Down These New Roads

A few years ago, as I was packing my bags for a late-night bus ride from New York City to Saint Louis, I realized that there was one item missing from my careful preparations: a book. Since I had already read all of the books at hand in my apartment, and the bus was due to leave in less than an hour, it was necessary that I make a quick purchase at a nearby bookstore.

Glancing at my watch as I checked the shelves, and finding little interest in any of the available books, I was about to give up when a title leaped out of my memory: Down These Mean Streets. Several friends had mentioned the book to me, insisting that I read it. They had described it as one of the few books which had given them the feeling that its author was holding nothing back; a true autobiography. I decided to take advantage of this opportunity to read it for myself and come to my own conclusions.

On the bus, along the way, my journey and that of Piri Thomas seemed to coalesce. As I gazed at the rolling landscape, he ran down Amsterdam Avenue; as I turned the pages, he turned the corners of those "mean streets" of his world. The clamor of his ghetto experience blended into the hum of my highways, late into the night. I can hardly remember the faces of the other passengers; a common listlessness seemed to transform them all into one anonymous, sleeping traveler. Night crawled up, in and out, lingering awhile before slipping into dawn. But I was still reading Down These Mean Streets. I really had no other choice.

Piri Thomas has written two other autobiographies: Savior, Savior, Hold My Hand, which outlines his work as a youth counselor in New York City; and Seven Long Times, a prison narrative which has been compared to the writings of Jean Genet. He is one of the founders of Third World Cinema, the film company that produced the popular movie, Claudine.

On my way to this interview, I reflected upon Piri Thomas as I perceived him through his books. He struck me as an accomplished writer, a poet and a craftsman. I believed that his work was honest; I believed that I knew him. But I couldn't determine to what degree Piri, or any writer, could achieve total honesty, total communication, with a huge public.

I met Hector outside the brownstone where the interview was to take place. After rapping a bit, we climbed the stairs to the third floor, and to the apartment where Piri Thomas, my companion on a bus ride a few years past, sat waiting.

Cal Wilson: What projects are you involved in right now? Do you have a novel in progress?

Piri Thomas: I'm involved in seven projects, and the novel is one of them. As a matter of fact, I've got three or four chapters written, but I haven't looked at it in a long time.

Cal: Would you agree that when Down These Mean Streets came out, the critics did not pay enough attention to your writing style and your writing ability and just dwelled on the subject matter?

Piri: As soon as I wrote the book, I jumped on my horse, following the wisdom of John Oliver Killens, who in a very beautiful sense was an inspiration for me to write in prison because I read his Youngblood in prison, and the thing is is that I did not gorge myself into it. I seem to remember being part of it, and I read it. John O. Killens said, hey, it's not enough just to write it, now you get on your horse and spread the word, and that's what I was doing, barn-storming, going where ever I could. Otherwise it would have been totally forgotten. But it crept in as a sleeper.

Hector Lino, Jr.: How many copies did Down These Mean Streets sell?

Piri: Oh, it sold. . .beaucoups. I still get some royalties but they're few and far between, because they have to sell a lot of books so that I can make a couple of thousands dollars. A lot of the people out there felt, hey, man you've made it now, millions are pouring in; and actually, the publishing houses get 85% of the deal. You get 15%, and out of that 15, when a paperback deal comes, you have to give away 7 ½; some even give more. Then you need an agent. . .because that's the only way they're going to publish your book. They say, well, if you want you book published, we get 85%.

Cal: Out of the remaining 15%, where does half of that go?

Piri: Well, out of the remaining 15% of a paperback deal, you get only 7 ½%. So usually, what you'd like is that a paperback version come out of it, because then more volumes will sell. People can afford to deal and will pay for a paperback. So what we do get is fame, but no bread.

Cal: Now, *Down These Mean Streets*

Piri: It had been banned, along with other books that were considered offensive by some. . .

Cal: By libraries, for example?

Piri: *Down These Mean Streets*, to my knowledge, had been banned in Salinas, California, and in Connecticut; it was banned in Teaneck, New Jersey, Virginia, and recently it had been banned in District 25 (NYC) and it was reinstated, just recently. After two years, they put it back into the library.

Cal: How does that work out legally?

Piri: They were dealing with it on the premises of obscenity. At one of those meetings. . .I attended as many as I could, and spoke my piece, not in defense of it, but in its right. Because it was a piece of life, it was written from the ink of life. I told them that anything can be taken out of context. . .that whole feeling of beauty is in the eye of the beholder. If you take the Bible out of context you're going to find a lot of things that could be misconstrued as offensive. But, that offensiveness only has to do with how small the person's understanding is.

Cal: Your first three books were autobiographies. . .

Piri: I wrote them in novel form, though. I read many books while I was in prison. I've forgotten many titles because after seven years. . .you're locked in your cell and if you've got something to read, you read. But the thing with *Down These Mean Streets* is that I wanted it to be as it was happening. I wanted people to see the sees and hear the hears and do the do's and walk the walks and talk the talk. I wanted it to be something like *Alice in Wonderland* with a ghetto kick. Where people go into that whole rap; pick up the book, and and that would be the closest thing to a moving picture. Because your mind, as you're reading, draws your imagery. I write in imagery; I write in descriptiveness and personal involvement. *Down These Mean Streets* was a work of the gut, and now I've learned how to work with the other essence also, the spirit of creativity.

Cal: How are you affected by people knowing so much about you, through reading your books, in terms of intimate experiences? Do you censor your writing?

Piri: Writing *Down These Mean Streets* was one of the toughest books that I've had to write, because it was actually, in a sense, my second. While I was in prison, and dealing with Muslim brothers within the prison walls, I found that beautiful spark of dignity that said, hey, this is where it is, my pecking order. That's why I moved very closely to the Muslim brothers. I learned and studied in the circle with a brother named Muhammad, and we got politically aware of what was happening. Even then in the fifties, because when the prison riot broke out in '55, it didn't break *out*; it broke off for food, but it had been very badly staged. Activists. . had to be careful, because they would get wasted in prison, immediately. These were the "troublemakers", and

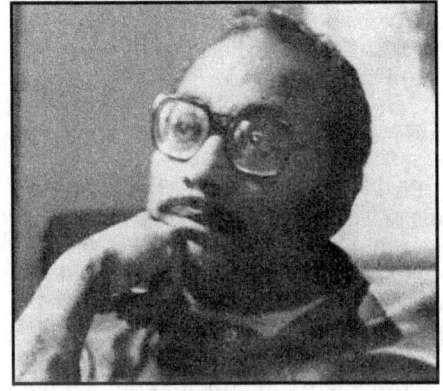

this was during the days of the McCarthy witch hunt. . . .

Hector: In which prison did the riot take place?

Piri: I was in Sing Sing and then from there got shipped to what is considered a maximum security prison, Comstock, or the Great Meadows Correctional Institution.

Hector: What was the charge?

Piri: Let me see if I can get it together in my mind. . .oh yes. You know, sometimes there's a distaste of going through certain things, but I've learned to deal with it very well. That's why I said *Down These Mean Streets* was very hard to write, 'cause it was out of my . . .actually a second book, but it was out of my pure guts. The charge was attempted armed robbery in the first degree, felonious assault with intent to kill, in the first degree. Then the Bronx wanted Manhattan to give me a probation on it, then try me as a second offender, immediately, in the Bronx. They wanted to lock the door on me for thirty to sixty years. Somehow, by some Providence, some human being there

with a sense of dignity said, "No, that is not the case. We will try him for this because this is where he was caught."

So, after I did my time, I went up on parole once and I was hit with two more years. When I went out again, they paroled me to these warrants. They came to the prison, and as they paroled me they put the cuffs on me, and handed me a whole bunch of letters that they didn't allow me to have from, I call her "Trina" in the book.

Cal: How did you cope with the pressure of being part of the prison population?

Piri: It was heavy because, too often, out of our frustration the stronger prisoners would turn on the weaker ones among us. We had to fight off that abnormal feeling. . .because each of us has latent tendencies towards homosexuality. I've always said, I'm half man and half woman, and I once said it out in the open, and I heard the murmur ran over that audience, "Old Petey's coming out" (laughs) And I say that I consider myself half-man and half-woman because how can I honor my father and negate my mother? I don't have the sense of ego to deal with this *machismo* bit. One thing I've analyzed about myself is that I work to correct, because life is a growing process.

Cal: Would you agree that being a writer gives you a certain amount of power?

Piri: Of course, writing is power. Just recently we ve had the passing of a very, very. . .transition, because to me he's not dead. And he was an incredible, beautiful, honorable, dignified, creative, human being. . .Paul Robeson. I remember at thirteen years old, I was sitting with a buddy of mine called Peelee, on top of Father Divine's shoe shine stand on 108th Street listening to an incredible voice singing. And it was Paul Robeson. I perhaps, did not understand his words, but I certainly understood his sincerity and his love. We have misplaced that sense of wisdom, of respecting those who have a feeling of giving, of understanding, listening to the words. I listen to children; I listen to older people; I listen to my peers, contemporaries, and I have I found that I learned, but only when I listened. Listened not to the words but to their meanings. I have a power, we all have a power. I will never write irresponsibly. I will never write to make the buck. I do not write that way.

Cal: What do you think the critics were saying with their response to **Savior, Savior**?

Piri: I wasn't writing to please them! I was writing the truth as I saw it. I was writing *Savior, Savior, Hold My Hand*, under incredible pressures, both personal, emotional, financial; all the human things that happen. I wanted that to come out much better. *Down These Mean Streets* could have come out much better. **Seven Long Times** could have come out much better. I make an analogy that each book is a child to me; that's as close as I will know of giving birth. When I have finished an essence that makes me say, "Vaya!" Then I set it to fly, man.

Cal: Then you're constantly growing in this writing?

Piri: Yes, because the danger is that you write something and then fall in love with it that you never do anything else; you just keep admiring it. I do remember this happening to many writers. When *Down These Mean Streets* first came out, man, I used to go from bookstore to bookstore to see it in the windows. I'd go in and I'd do a number. Like if somebody would have it in their hand, reading it, dealing with it, and I'd say (clears throat) "That is a fine book," and then I'd say, "You read it? I wrote it." (laughs) Hey, why not, I'm human. Of course, now I don't have to do that, but when you've gone through so many rejects in your whole lifetime, it's nice to let this little light of mine shine, and I wasn't doing it with arrogance. I had that certain want to do it, because the people that I always approached were going there. . .because I wanted them to know that this wasn't something that they wrote for me. They were passing out rumors that I had a ghost writer. Listen, the idea is, because of this society and how it is and its racist bit, all these pressures either makes you super bad or super shit. . . And I certainly feel, without modesty, that I'd like to be super bad, but without arrogance. Many times you can take the power that pins you down and write something that will destroy it. It's not that you tell the truth; it's how you tell it. I can tell a truth that will inform you, educate you, or kill you, and I can tell it in a way that it will inform and uplift. Hey, when I wrote it, I didn't know that the reaction was going to be that much. I didn't take myself that seriously as a writer. To take yourself seriously as a writer is an accomplishment indeed. And then you don't want to do nothing else. No matter if you're broke. You write, because if you don't write, it builds up in you, and frustration sets in. We must do what we have to do! If human beings cannot express themselves, they get all turned inside and then become so hate-filled that their creativity is all negative, man. The power of writing, the power of art, . . . music, art, writing, plays, everything that is art communicates to all, if all would look and listen.

Cal: I'd like to get into the novel that you're writing. . .

Piri: I've written three autobiographies. I am now involved in writing a novel and it's a labor of love. I'm dealing with it because, hey, I don't want no interruptions when I'm writing. I'm serious about that. The work involved is not writing it out; it is the thinking it out. The knitting it, breathing it. So I have a very imaginative mind; give me a situation, I'll deal with it.But now, to do something is not enough, is what I'm saying. To know what you're doing: that's the answer. So if you're sure of yourself, it's beautiful, you know what I mean? How can I put it? I have a genuine sense of balance. I've had to in order to walk between the raindrops. And when I was a kid, people would say, hey, man, Petey, don't be too beautiful, they'll kill you. And I could understand; I understood the meaning of the danger, and that makes me more determined to be beautiful.

Cal: I believe the title of your novel is, *The Man Who Spins The Web.*

Piri: Yeah, that's a tentative title. That is only a tentative title.

Cal: Was it necessary for you to write those autobiographies in order to get past those experiences. . .

Piri: Well, the reason, I'd been wanting to get these three books out of my guts and my heart, and my spirit, and hey, I did it my way, you know, and I got it out. I knew that if I didn't get it out, for the rest of my life I'd be writing about ghetto, ghetto, ghetto, ghetto, ghetto, ghetto, ghetto, and there's more to the world than ghetto. And this novel is beautiful, man. But remember what I'm saying. There are many different forms of writing. You don't write a novel like I wrote *Down These Mean Streets* yet that's the same format. So in a novel. . . .

Hector: By format, what do you mean?

Piri: It's a similar format, because instead of writing an autobiography, like saying, I did this and I did that, I'd involve other people and feelings. I made this in a novel form of autobiography, because I'm more gifted toward descriptiveness and narrative and setting and stage and moves. But now, with this novel, I've just finished reading two or three chapters that I've already written, and it starts in the mountains of Puerto Rico. Hey, man, that's the writing I want to deal with. It's beautiful, and it's creative. I can fly. I've found that when I'm into it, all of a sudden, I am not just writing; I'm part of it, man, and the characters take on lives of their own.

Cal: When dealing with a social theme, what would you say is the effect of a fictional, as opposed to a non-fictional, approach, in terms of reaching an audience.

Piri: Are you asking me which is the most important?

Cal: Which do you feel has the greater impact on the greater amount of people?

Piri: I have to say it in my way. When I was fifteen years old, I went to the Merchant Marines because I wanted to see the world. So I lied and signed aboard a Greek ship, under the Panamanian flag, and said I was a second fireman, thinking it was running on oil, and ended up shoveling coal; you know, two thousand years before the mast, (laughs) and no law except survival. They were killers on that ship, and you had to be heavy. I tackled a Swede one time, about six feet three, and I was so damn scared, I didn't know how to kill him. But I had him; I was stronger, but somehow I just didn't want to kill him, 'cause it would have been brutality. And so, what I'm telling you, in reply to your question, is that every 360° of understanding and knowledge are needed, for unity. In a Puerto Rican anthology of all the history of Puerto Rico, it says, well, Piri Thomas' book has a lot of validity, but it doesn't give a clear picture of what it's all about, and their book does —which, of course it does! I wrote about a specific lifestyle, a feeling; I'm a historian and a recorder. Some of my poetry has been coming out in different books, and I have an anthology of poetry called *Sounds From The Street* I feel my blackness, I feel my heritage that's puertoriqueno, I feel my humanity, It's not a matter of color; it's a matter of spirit.

Cal: If I write a scholarly treatment of something. . . .

Piri: Scholars will read it.

Cal: But if I write a novel, that's on the shelves right next to *Jaws*, wouldn't you agree that it would have more of an impact?

Piri: The idea is to write in 360 degrees, so that you reach all levels and all people. And the way you do it is that you write about something that is relevant to them; you strike chords; you get to know other ethnic groups. I was a loner. And I'd go down South, and I'd down here, and go down there, and get to know people. How can you know people unless you get to them on a one-to-one basis? I'm not a writer that will write out of what somebody tells me. I've got to see it with my own beautiful brown eyes. I've got to smell it, and taste it. I'm now working on a screenplay. I'm one of the founders of Third World Cinema. We were responsible for *Claudine*. The screenplay, which I'm writing for Third World Cinema, deals

Cont'd on page 54

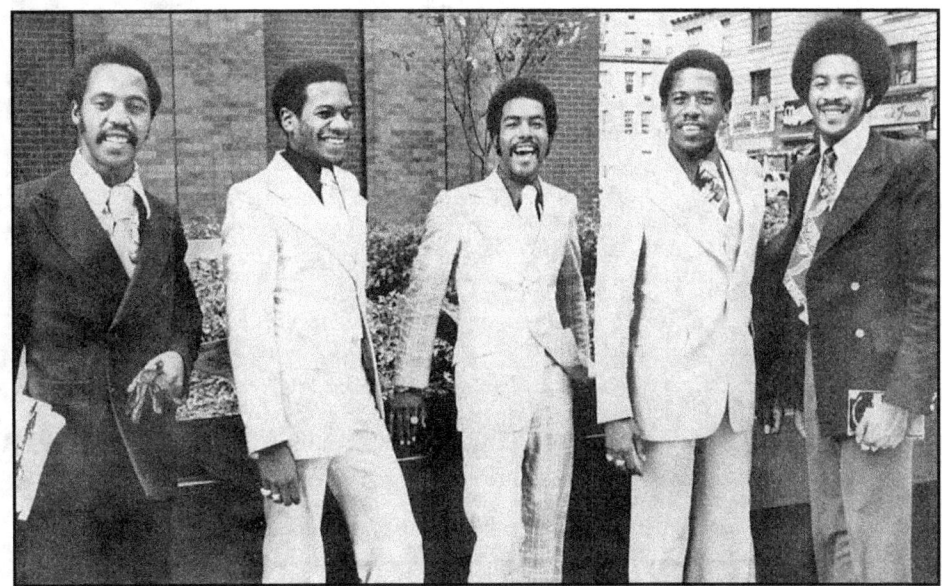

Photo courtesy Atlantic Records

BLUE MAGIC:

Philly Soul

Watching BLUE MAGIC perform was for me a culmination of many private moments spent alone with my thoughts and with their magical sounds that had miraculously transformed my home into a bouquet of emotional colours.

As they cast a positive spell, I was enchanted, listening and feeling their moments of reality, the beauty of love, unity and the understanding expressed by the five melodious voices of Philadelphia.

BLUE MAGIC is more than just five elegant gentlemen who have mastered their craft and with gentle genius blended together to produce harmony. Blue Magic's appeal is universal, projecting love and unity to all who listen and watch. "Anytime that you have five different people, you have what we call 'reaching common ground', and in our case the common denominator is that we have the same idea about reaching the people: singing about what life is all about."

Ted Mills, lead singer of the group, further elaborates, "Knowing that men fall in love with women, and that not everybody talks about it; it's an experience. But when something comes on that relates to something that they have personally experienced or might have heard about, it's meaningful for them and it helps them to establish lines of communication and understanding."

By expressing the deepest of personal experiences understood by all of humanity, Blue Magic becomes, in the profoundest sense of the word, communicators. And communicate they did, as a packed Felt Forum sang, clapped hands and patted their feet with the popular quintet and the familar sound of Philly. "Being felt in the audiences— that's what you can call the mystical element, the spiritual contact that you create through your audience. It doesn't matter how big that audience is."

In less than three years Blue Magic have become one of the top male vocal groups in the world today. Magic. . . truly. . .yet possessed with a keen sense of the practical aspects of show business. "We've gone through the transition of getting to know what show business is all about. When you begin, you have ideas about what it's all about, but it takes experience to know, and that takes time. We've moved into produc-

ing our own product and selecting our songs, and we have a business which is called Blue Magic and a part of that is MYSTIC DRAGON."

Working together as an act and as business partners, Vernon Sawyer, Richard Pratt, Wendell Sawyer, Keith Beaton and Ted Mills coordinate a publishing firm, including a staff of attorneys and accountants, in which each member participates and functions as competent business partners. They understand that solvency is necessary in order to keep the creative product to their liking and preserve its integrity.

On their latest album, *Thirteen Blue Magic Lane*, Mystic Dragon produced the tracks *Chasin' Rainbows*, *I Like You*, and *What's Come Over Me*, all penned by the "WIZARD", Ted Mills.

In addition to all this, Blue Magic works with some of the most creative producers and arrangers in the business: Norman Harris, Ron "Have Mercy" Kersey, Bobby Eli, Ronnie Baker and Earl Young. Coupled with the incomparable Sigma Sound Studios and

Article by Bob Bryan from an interview by Bob Bryan and Michael Jamison
complemented by the MAGIC OF THE BLUE [their back-up band], tell me, how can you lose?

The knowledge that has emerged from such an excellent collaboration of talents has given Blue Magic an insight into the business that normally would have taken over 20 years to learn. Twenty years of knowledge in three years is a huge step forward.

Possessing the talent and self-confidence which is needed to succeed, Blue Magic has learned that the only thing that stands between your vision and reality are the trials, tribulations and hardships of life. "If you can learn to govern your actions in an affirmative way, you can learn to control your destiny and your future,. . .and that all fits into a pattern of correct living. That's sort of what the message is all about. . .this business requires discipline, because you've got to do things that you don't want to do. But you have got to follow through with your commitments in order to accomplish your goals." ✿

"Rhythm is life the space of time danced thru."

--Cecil Taylor

The National Black Theater is a place of celebration, a temple where life takes on the shape of the spirit's imaginings. There is no stage here, and no spectators; the space itself is the experience, as warm rushes of energy called "preacher rhythms" wash over everyone involved. It is a ceremony of joy and love, inspired by Barbara Ann Teer.

As director of the National Black Theater, Barbara AnnTeer has led her company away from conventional concepts of acting and theater, venturing into new forms and ideas. Through observations, experimentation and research, she has created "ritualistic revivals" which project her vision of the Black community and its diverse lifestyles.

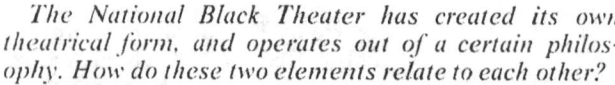

Barbara Ann Teer
and
The National Black Theater

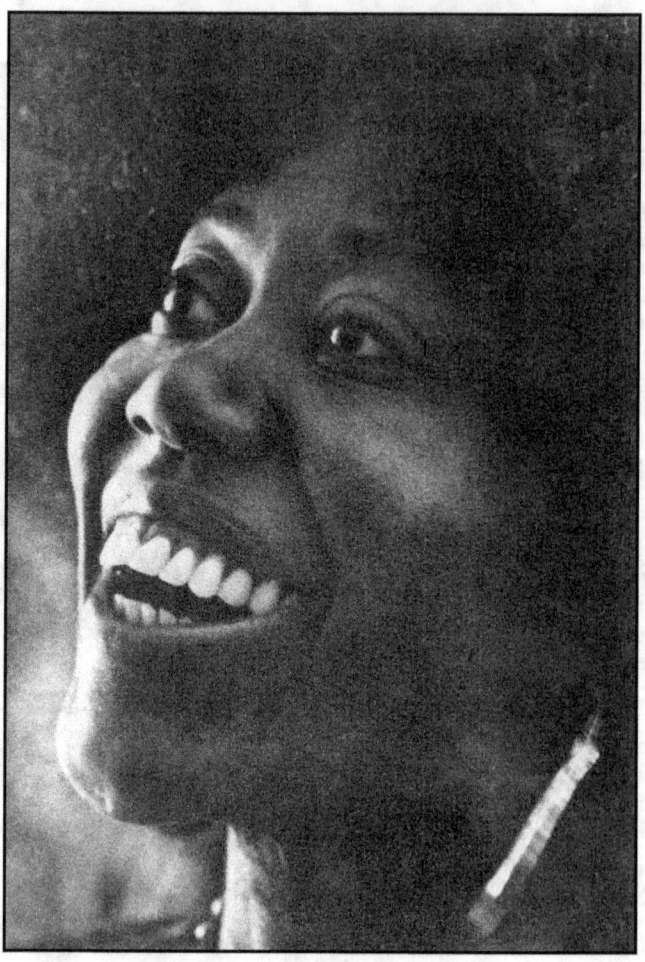

The National Black Theater has created its own theatrical form, and operates out of a certain philosophy. How do these two elements relate to each other?

The National Black Theater is really not a theater; it's much more than a theater. We use that name because it's identifiable with Black people. Most people have expectations about the word "theater." And since it does have a lot of charge on it, the word "theater," in relationship to entertainment and leisure and recreation, it's easier to develop audiences around the title "theater." I've thought for years about changing that title, and I've just not done it. The National Black Theater is one aspect of a permanent Black institution in Harlem. Theater, if it were properly defined, is a place or space of reeducation. It doesn't have to be inside or in a particular type of building. Theater for me is simply a vehicle for reeducation. So the institution becomes a center of communication, a temple of liberation, and, as we say in our revival, sometimes it is a theater for a Black nation. People have put a lot of charge on words, as far as the particular ideology which all art flows from. And that ideology is the ideology which flows from the religous base of the society. All societies have basic foundations which provide values and guidelines as to how people grow and develop, and out of that particular ideology which is translated into values and guidelines comes a culture which reflects those values and guidelines. In turn, out of that cultural entity come different types of art forms, and these art forms simply reflect the culture which reflects the religious system. If you look at that scientifically, when I left commercial, Western theater, Broadway, it was very clear to me that what I was doing in theater was not satisfying my inner needs, my spiritual growth, my need to develop as a human being, my need to become. My potential was not developing in a way that I wanted it to. So the first thing I did was close the doors on all the things I'd ever learned, the degrees, the university, the awards, so that I could go into myself. There are no book or films that deal with the African experience or the Black experience, the experience which I know through being brought up in a Black community. I went internally, I went into myself, and I devised what I call a Black Art Standard. That standard is based on observation, experimentation, research; witnessing all events and experiences that happen in Harlem, from the church, such as the Holy Roller Pentecostal churches, to the Apollo, to bars, to pool rooms, to barber shops. Just sitting there, day after day, observing the tonal qualities and rhythms of the language, the way people walk, and the attitudes of people. From that we developed what we call "the five cycles of evolution." We teach a class called "Cycles" which deals with the total summation of those five cycles: the nigger cycle, the negro cycle, the militant cycle, the nationalist cycle, and the revolutionary cycle. It took us two years to develop sound technique excercises, facts, data, experiences and processes that would allow Black people to go through these different cycles of conscious-

16

ness and analyze how they have been affected by the Western system. None of these cycles we named ourselves, but all of them were defined and put on us, and we became the implementors of those so-called titles. So the new standard was developed; the next step was to develop a new form to house this standard. The form that I developed was called "rituals." And, as we say in the piece, a ritual is a reverent rite marking the passing from one space to a more highly evolved space. Our first ritual was done on *Soul*, which was at that time on national television , produced by Ellis Haizlip. That ritual was done and got 1,000 phone calls the first night, and it was re-done back to back three times in succession and out of that the National Black Theater became an entity. At first we didn't have a space large enough to perform in, so we went to the Apollo and performed on a bill with Little Richard, and it was phenomenal. We got a lot of offers to do TV, but they were all commercial and Western kinds of things. I refused those offers because I had not refined and perfected the ritual to the degree that I controlled it. If you have something that's innovative and exciting, and put it out there for the mass media to see, the next thing you know it's everywhere. You can't control it and you don't get any credit for devising or developing it. We began to perform and perfect the ritual, and what we have now is a form we call "revival." And so that people don't get confused with "revival" meaning "play revival" or "church revival", we call them "ritualistic revivals." Our form basically comes from taking the church form and making it a more theatrical experience. We use "preacher rhythms" because they are charismatic and automatically get people's energy up. Just as, in his day, Shakespeare used iambic pentameter to relate the folk language, we use a certain kind of rhythm to relate to Black folks' language. And our institution has three full-time programs: a Blackening program on Sundays; an educational program which includes workshops covering all kinds of subjects, from men's groups, women's groups, and men-women groups, to workshops on movement, evolutionary movement, liberation cycles, and how to create miracles; and we have the performing unit. I'm going to teach a new series this year called "Living Out The Lie Of Oppression." We have a workshop called "Black Cultural Pace-Setters" which includes people like John Henrik Clarke, and which deals with history. We have workshops in Yoruba religious cultures, and these workshops run every night. We have children's workshops, and creative expression workshops. The performing unit is the unit that takes the ideology and puts it into theatrical form, so that the ideology can manifest itself in the people that perform it, as well as the people in the community who witness it. We don't have audiences; we have participants. And we try to make it one big family, one big congregation, wherein everyone gets a chance to experience his or her perfection.

Please describe the "decrudding" process and its relationship to the five cycles of evolution.

The "decrudding" process does just what it says—it removes from your mind the blocks and the barriers, the programming, that comes as a direct result of being trained in schools based on European concepts of education. There are no African or African-American institutions in the world. They all come from a European or a Western base. So when we speak of "decrudding", we mean that before we can talk about an African experience or an African-American experience, we must first deal with what is. And that is, we are all steeped in American thinking—Western images and Western ideologies. The "decrudding" process gives you an opportunity to move through those ideological positions and be clear about what they are, to look at the blocks and barriers you have, the resistance you have; it allows you to experience yourself as an African-American and alter or demolish those programmed images about who we are. And in the West, we are clearly "inadequate", "inferior", "oppressed"; all these words that have been laid on us. Black people believe themselves to be oppressed, to be inferior, so they resist what really is. And they work so hard to prove that that's a lie, when in fact it is, so you don't have to prove yourself, you just move in a different way. I would like to add, in reference to your original question about the ideology, that I am clear that we do not have racial problems. We come from different paths of evolution, and because we come from different evolutionary paths, we experience ourselves differently. See, the West is the West and the East is the East. They're not the same. One goes from outside, in; the other, from inside, out. And it's just that simple. I don't need to say any more about it. One is circular; one is square. One deals with space and with spiritual substance, and the other deals with time and form. Black people are usually very frightened of form, and Europeans are very frightened of experience and space. And that's how I see the problem. It has nothing to do with color. It has nothing to do with images that there's somebody who has more than I have. We both have the same thing; we approach it differently. People considered African countries as poor, but they simply have different intensions and they don't experience themselves the way we do.

How would you describe your relationship to Pan-Africanism?

Well, "pan" means "all," and I relate to all African people the same way I relate to myself. If you're talking about the political aspect or the cultural aspect, and they shouldn't be split, I am an African woman who was born in America. Which means I have African-American experiences, and I am totally in line with anything that deals with the subject of African people. In 1973, because of my frustration in trying to reach people and tell them that what we were doing would create an evolutionary change for Black people, I chose to go to Africa. The first time I went to Africa, I went on a Ford Foundation fellowship. I stayed for four months and I built a base in Oshobo, Nigeria I came back with some Nigerians—one of them was Twins Seven Seven, who is an internationally famous artist and musician. He has his own band. And I brought back from America to Africa my entire theater company, and we stayed over there for two months. We built a base—we put in the plumbing, the kitchens and everything. What we wanted to do was start an international Pan-African cultural complex. When we got back to this country we brought back five more Nigerians. What stopped the project was the economic thing. We could not raise the money to build a cultural base in Harlem with an extension in Nigeria. And because of that the brothers went back and we began to re-focus our attention on being African-American and not African-Pan-African people.

How did you use the Black family structure as a model in organizing the National Black Theater?

I didn't; it was just the natural process of evolution. Once you're clear what the source is, things just fall into place. You see, there are all kinds of philosophies and ideologies put out, by Black men particularly, about the role of the Black family, and the role of the Black man, and I found them all confining and restricting. I also found them very frustrating as a Black woman, and I take total responsibility for nurturing all Black minds. When I say that, I don't mean me individually. All Black minds are molded out of the womb of a Black woman; therefore, anything I don't like I take responsibility for, rather than complaining and bitching about it. I began to analyze and try to get to the source of it. It was satisfying for me to accept someone else's point of view based on their programming from their mothers, so rather than talk about the things I didn't like, I looked for the things I did like and really wanted. I went to Africa and spent time with African religious leaders, priests, and priestesses. I was initiated into quite a few different cults. Whenever I have a question, I just put it out there in my head and the answers come. The company went to Africa for the Oshun festival. Oshun is the goddess of harmony and love and fertility, and she's a very powerful deity, when we came back, we wee all very clear about what we had to do—bring children into the world. And that's what we chose to do. The brothers were all very much a part of it, and very excited about it. Before that, we had a family organization, but the whole dimension and depth of that organization changed when we began to bring children into the world. We're very excited about that. We now have eight children in the National Black Theater; they run from eighteen months to five weeks old, and it's totally turned the whole structure of the institution around.

How do you feel about "liberators" taking roles in the commercial theater while they are still associated with NBT?

I feel it's very good, although I don't like judgements of "good" or "bad". Anything a person can do to enhance his or her experience of who they are, is a plus. "Commercial" is just a word. I'd like everyone in the National Black Theater to be exposed to the maximum to the Western medium and audience, so that they can get to experience total perfection, total godliness. The people of the National Black Theater come from a space of grace; they've been trained to come from a space of grace. When they set foot on any kind of platform, their presences are so electrifying —it comes out of a space of divinity— until it just raises people's consciousness. So I don't like to get into "commercial" or "non-commercial" —I would like people to be exposed to the National Black Theater. Whenever anybody goes out of the National Black Theater, they're still there, because that's their home, their family and their base. Whenever anybody goes out, it only makes NBT more visible, because people get to see from the program, "Hey, that person was trained by the NBT, that must be a dynamite place, let me go check it out." So, in essence, it increases our visibility. It also improves our financial situation, because we are not a financially solvent institution at this point. But we still manage to maintain ourselves. I think it's fantastic when people work outside of the NBT, because they are working for us.

Do you plan to go "commercial"?

Cont'd on page 51

How She Got Over

By Ernell Elizabeth Worrell

Marilyn Betsey Cummings had matured as a paranoid; she had had lots of help. Still, she was now 34 years old, and she tried to think more positively, and to speak more positively, in order that she not appear too unlike the ordinary person. On the other hand, since her 20th birthday, she had been in a mental hospital four times. She believed, however, that she would never again have to be put into an institution. She believed this because she knew that, according to the life that she had been living prior to her 29th year (the last time she had been committed) she was presenting an entirely new "profile."

She also believed that she had a long life ahead, and she had in the making all-new approaches to old problems, the first being that she was left out of most of the living that Black woman her age were getting done. She could recall herself reckoning with this problem since she was seven years old, and even younger. She had come to believe that people didn't want her around. She attributed this to the fact that most people are afraid to be needed. Thus, she had lived a slower, more intense life than the average Black child her age, and now she was living a slower, more intense life that the average Black woman her age. Yet, at the age of twelve, she had decided to make every minute of her life count. She had determined to approach it, therefore, seriously and meaningfully. She had time and again worn out her pitiful, lonely brain, trying to function thusly. She could recall that once, when she was nineteen, she had written:

> *"Let me be,*
> *For just an instant,*
> *Free*
> *Among the living*
> *Full of warmth,*
> *And hope."*

This inner plight was perhaps her prayer to Fate for life, but at that time she was thankful to "mercy" that she had gotten over childhood.

Marilyn had been called "homely" in her time; she also had several appearance defects. For instance, until July of 1975, she had had only six bottom teeth in her entire mouth. At the end of November, 1974, the year past, she had broken a hook off the bottom half of her plate. The upper portion of the plate, which comprised an entire bridge, had always wobbled, so she could not wear it either. Doctor Steven M. Weisburg had been her dentist. He had done a perfect, inexpensice job. She had promised herself that she would have him to make up an entire plate again, someday soon. That is, a more expensive one. Then, during the spring, on May 14, to be precise, Doctor Alvin H. Harris had performed reconstructive surgery on what had been a scarred, fat upper-left side portion of her lip. It had not appeared as natural in size since she was eleven years old. She had at that time endured an almost fatal swing accident.

When she was twelve, she began to wear prescription glasses. She hoped that they would conceal the sadness of the hurt, unloved expression in her dark brown eyes. At fifteen, she would gaze into her bedroom mirror, wondering how she was seen in the eyes of others, particularly, those of young men of her community. As a teen she would also sit in the hot sun, hoping to darken her brown skin. She had imagined herself to be a yellowish color. Now, she could see the reddish highlights of her skin tone. Since 1970, she had worn wigs. During the summer of 1968, she had cut off the remaining four inches of her soft, thin, off-black hair. With this year, it had grown out from a quarter-of-an-inch to eight or nine uneven inches. On November 8, she had gone to "Joseph," a leading beautician for permanents. He had personally hacked off about three inches, for practice sake. She was in the process of balding because of the chemical ingredients of the permanent, which was devised by Revlon, until she decided to see trichologist Mr. Mosely, of Dermalax System, Incorporated, on December 9. Finally, at 30, she had decided to gain weight. She had lost down to a "regular" size 18, with measurements of 40-34-42. Since she was 15 years old, her weight had ranged between 105 to 115 pounds, but she had come to weigh as much as 187. She was 5' 3". Thus, she was not as perfect as she had occasionally beheld herself. After all, there had simply been no one to tell her differently. Still, when she was eighteen, her mother would tell her that she was boney, and looked "bad." Otherwise, when she was happy, she would look into the mirror, and see loveliness, but when she was sad, she saw what she feared everyone else saw. Now, she had the confidence of steel. Besides, she had reasoned out a philosophy on "beauty." At twenty she had written: "Beauty is uniqueness." And she believed.

Marilyn Betsey had lived with her mother, Teresa Kate, all of her life. Her mother had left her father, Clarence, after the birth of her sister Anna Josephine. Marilyn was then a year-and-a-half old. Her mother had filled her life so much that the longing which she always had for her father was more instinctive than requested. This made her happy, now that she could understand the fear, loneliness,, and torture that her mother had endured in trying to raise she and her sister without him. Marilyn had vowed that she would put off marriage until a man cared for her enough to want to work for their children. She knew that perhaps this would never be. However, she had come to believe that the average Black man would never care enough for her to work for her or their children, and she didn't want a White man.

Teresa Kate, or "Kay", as Marilyn had called her since she was six, was a small woman. Her beautiful, bright, childishly happy eyes had dulled with her 52 years. She preferred to tint those strands of off-black hairs that were turning gray. Her sense of humor was a tease. For many years, she never talked about her unhappiness to either of her daughters. She was old-fashioned, and platonic. She believed in providing for her children, first; they never saw a hungry day. She had sour words for all men, however, and from the time the girls were ten years old, she shared her thoughts with Marilyn and Anna almost daily. Kay had worked as a domestic when she first brought Marilyn and Anna to New York City. Since June, 1956, however, she had worked as a therapeutic aide at Brooklyn State Hospital. *Cont'd on page* 42

BLACK PICTURE SHOW

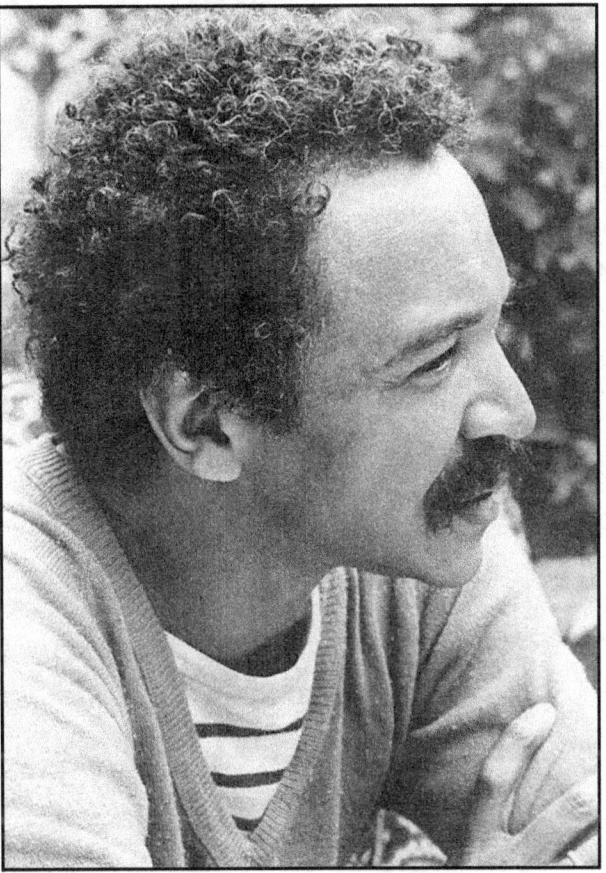

Playwright, Bill Gunn.

Black Picture Show, *a play by Bill Gunn, was performed to critical acclaim at Lincoln Center. Briefly, the play was a poetic surrealistic depiction of the problems of the Black artist in this society.*

Presented here is an excerpt from Black Picture Show, *published by Reed, Cannon and Johnson.*

ORIGINAL CAST

(in order of appearance)

VOCALIST.................................... SAM WAYMON
J.D., Alexander's son........................ALBERT HALL
ALEXANDER, a Black Artist
                       DICK ANTHONY WILLIAMS
HOSPITAL ATTENDANTS............. WILLIAM LEET,
                               MARVIN BECK
NORMAN, Alexander's companion GRAHAM BROWN
ARNOLD, Alexander's father....... GRAHAM BROWN
LILY, Alexander's mother................. CAROL COLE
RITA, Alexander's second wife........... CAROL COLE
PHILIPPE, a movie producer PAUL-DAVID RICHARDS
JANE, Philippe's wife......................LINDA MILLER

19

(As the lights come up we see the room now softly lit. It is empty. The living room set with flowers. Candles aglow. A few of the pieces of old furniture have been replaced with modern pieces. Chrome and plexiglass reflect the glowing fire from the fireplace. The dining table is beautifullly set. The best china and crystal is set. Fresh candles are on the table unlit. Liquor and glasses are set out along the sideboard. Soft smooth bossa nova lingers in the room, it seems a continuation of the music last heard in the last scene. The house is now well dressed aglow.
RITA enters, ALEX's wife. SHE is a well-dressed Black woman. Very well dressed. SHE carries a canvas traveling bag. SHE seems by her manner to be able, as one might say, to take care of herself. SHE is beautiful, in her thirties. Not the least bit ethnically attired. SHE has a tendency towards glamor, but SHE enhances it with her own down to earth thing.)

RITA

ALEX! ... ALEX! ... Damn it! NORMAN! ...

ALEXANDER

(Running out!)
I couldn't get the car started.

RITA

I took a cab.

ALEXANDER

I'm sorry.

RITA

From the airport ...

ALEXANDER

Well, I had you paged.

RITA

I'm starved ... I've got to get dressed ... give me a drink.

ALEXANDER

What do you want? I think I'll finish my play by New Year's.

RITA

Rum something with Rum ... I saw the sons of bitches on the train ... I met them when you were in Mexico ... You know, the lunch I wore that Scott Barrie dress ... What could I say. We need the money. Are you high?

ALEXANDER

(Getting her a drink)
I said I've almost finished my play!

RITA

He's going to ask you to do the picture. Do it!

ALEXANDER

Oh my dear ... Norman fixed the whole mess and left. He says it just takes heating. He's picked the table setting ...

RITA

I wanted to do that ...

ALEXANDER

It's alright. I told him to be pretentious ...

RITA

They're very *real* people ... They got your whole Nigga chic thing together so drop it.

ALEXANDER

With very real money.

RITA

They're going to the Persian Room to see Ethel Ennis, so they'll be dressed, so I think we should dress so they won't feel conspicuous.

ALEXANDER

You're so full of so many different kinds of shit ...

RITA

LISTEN BUSTER ... THIS IS SOMETHING I'M DOING FOR YOU! I COULD HAVE GONE STRAIGHT TO NEW YORK WITH THEM! But when I talked about my unemployed ... writer-genius-husband sitting home writing the great American nothing! ... He said I'd like to talk to him. Actually, he wants to get laid ... so I lead him to you, sugar face. J.D. wrote me you were in the hospital again. That's twice this month.

ALEXANDER

You understand that part of it. But I don't want to talk about it. I'm fine. Tip-top. Feel like writin' my ass off.

RITA

What do you want, some kind of passive bitch who'll let you starve? ... I've got too much respect for you to leave you where I found you.

ALEXANDER

Your process is going home ... You look like you're cracking.

RITA

Alex, I love you, but I don't want to sleep with you any more.

ALEXANDER

You got it baby.

RITA

You give me too much ... You overdo everything. I know it's good, but I'm sick of it ... O.K.

ALEXANDER

That's a load off my mind.
        (Laughs at his own joke)

RITA

I just want to run around a little bit outside ... your jurisdiction. I keep hoping somebody will love me ... I wished the cab driver would love me. He was attractive, but I think he was a cop.

ALEXANDER

You better get dressed. The cab driver. You're always cruising the god-damned cab driver.

RITA

Do you still love me?

ALEXANDER

I don't want to talk about it.

RITA

You could consider it ... I'm not at all trying to assert my rights. I'm suffering. I don't want to sleep with you and it worries me because I love you.

ALEXANDER

And I said alright! ... as I would to any ace boon coon.

RITA

I'm sorry.

ALEXANDER

JESUS CHRIST YOU HAVE TO BE TOLD SO MUCH! Why are we married? You talked me into that fucking contract.

RITA

Well ... take it or leave it. What shall we do tonight on ... Cocktails or reefers?

ALEXANDER

They're your guests, baby.

RITA

They're so White.

ALEXANDER

What do you mean so White?

RITA

I mean they're into such a heavy White thing. They live White, breathe White. They are White. White, White, White.

ALEXANDER

Norman made Coquilles Saint-Jacques ... and a quiche ... that should assure them ... It'll keep them from eating us.

RITA

Are you sure they go together?

ALEXANDER

The quiche? Don't worry. ... I don't give a damn. It's what Norman felt like doing. His mother had a White maid. . .

        (HE looks at her)
Darling glitter ... I love you when you glitter ... someting outrageous.

RITA

I thought to wear something simple.

ALEXANDER

Darling if you look like the Duchess of Windsor, they won't give us the job. Look just a little cheap for me dear. Remember, there's always the sensual promise. Without that you're just Black. Just a little cheap ... We need the money.

RITA
(Close to his lips and softly seductive)
Darling, it's the DeValois, not Judith Christ.

ALEXANDER

I'm going to eat you up when they leave.

RITA

Not unless I eat you first ... Then we must give me a break ... you really must let me have a lover.

ALEXANDER

You mean you don't have one already. You can have two or more ... not one. I'll get jealous if you have only one. If you were having an affair with one man I'd kill you. You can fuck. But no affairs.

RITA
(In a little whining voice like a baby)
Stop! ... I wasn't asking permission, man. I'd like your cooperation, that's all.
        (SHE kisses him long, HE responds)
I'll be dressed in a flash.
(SHE runs off.
ALEXANDER climbs the stairs as the bedroom lights come up.
NORMAN is laying out his tuxedo.) Cont'd on page 58

What is a song?

One definition holds that a song is "a musical setting for a poem." Based upon that statement, one thing is clear: Oscar Brown, Jr. is a master songwriter. Since writing his first recorded song, Brown Baby, twenty-five years ago, Brown has created a body of work which stands in rich affirmation to his genius. He has set words to the music of Miles Davis (All Blues) and Mongo Santamaria (Afro-Blue), and has written his own music to complement the poetry of Paul Laurence Dunbar and Gwendolyn Brooks.

A song is also "a composition to be rendered by the voice," and during the course of his career as a performer, Oscar Brown, Jr. has proven that his voice can ably interpret any song with a rare clarity of technique and depth of feeling. HIs recent engagement at Reno Sweeney in New York City was marked by standing-room-only crowds night after night, as audiences reacted enthusiastically to Brown's distinctive blend of humor, theatrics and musical skill.

Oscar Brown, Jr. has received international acclaim. Among the artists who have recorded his songs are Diana Ross, Nina Simone, B.B. King, Lou Rawls, Diahann Carroll and Al Wilson. Brown received critical praise for his musicals Kicks and Company , Joy *and* Buck White. *As a recording artist, his albums include* Movin' On, Fresh *and* Brother Where Are You. *on the Atlantic label.*

Cal Wilson: How do you go about the process of developing your songs?

Oscar Brown, Jr.: Well, there's no one way. It depends upon the song, and the circumstances under which I deal with it. For example, if I'm doing something for a play, or a specific musical, then I have to deal with the characters that are in that musical. I might have to write a character-development song, or one that will reveal to the audience what the character is feeling, musically. Or, I might need to do one that will musically reveal some action in the play; because that will put a certain kind of requirement upon it. That's when Im writing towards a specific project. If I'm writing children's songs, then that becomes the direction of my creative thought. But if I'm doing something on my own. . . .I might walk down the street and hear a phrase, or something will happen in my life that will cause me to respond emotionally.

Bob Bryan: So there's no set pattern?

Oscar: Right, there is no set way in which things are created. It depends upon the project and the purpose.

Bob: Is there a particular line that ties most of your work together?

Oscar: I'm not able to discern that. I'm told by musicians, of course, that I tend musically to deal with minor mode a lot. I just hear that melodically; I don't have any musical training. I don't read music. I make up tunes in my head and put them on tape, or have someone notate them for me. As far as the lyric aspect of it is concerned, the only thing that I try to do is the best I can. As far as each song is concerned, sometimes I overwrite. I've found it difficult to write, sometimes, for what is considered to be the popular market. Even though I really am writing for the popular market, I find it difficult to write in the form that most of the people who deal with the popular market are using. I tend to overwrite my songs as far as that market is concerned. By that, I mean, I get too elaborate in the lyrics, or I get

OSCAR BROWN JR. MOVIN' ON

too involved in the poetry of the thing, in the alliteration.

Bob: Who do you perceive as being your audience?

Oscar: Well, anybody I can get to. I mean, the whole world. The business of determining audiences is something that is usually imposed upon you by the business people. They are merchandisers of things and they quite often want to know, "Well, what kind of singer are you?" "What kind of performer are you?" They have to try to put you into a category. Not because they necessarily want to be bad fellows, or narrow-minded about it. It's just that you're much easier to sell if they know what kind of product you are. So if they can say, "He's a jazz singer; he's a folk singer; he's a blues singer," it makes it easier for them.

Bob: How have they been categorizing **you**?

Oscar: I haven't been categorized. I find it very difficult to categorize myself, and nobody else has been able to come up with anything that seems to satisfy what everyone wants in that department.

Cal: In terms of delivery, how do the stage versions of your songs differ from the recorded versions?

Oscar: Well, of course you are communicating with an audience as opposed to standing in a booth somewhere, as you do in a studio. I go through the changes, most fundamentally, of an actor.

Bob: Responding to the audience. . .

Oscar: Well, not necessarily; an actor doesn't do that. An actor comes out of the character, and digs into the character.

Bob: Some actors have said that they can feel out the audience and in that way determine how best to deliver their lines.

Oscar: Well no, not exactly. Yeah, there's some of that. There are obviously some dynamics that you get off an audience. A very enthusiastic audience, that's on your side, kicks you along; an audience that's cold and still makes it more difficult for you. But on the other hand, the audience is my responsibility. I have to assume that I promised to entertain them; they didn't promise to be entertained (laughed), they just promised to come and see. So, it is my responsibility to entertain the audience. I don't exactly fix my performance on the audience. I fix my performance on the performance, on what it has to be, itself. And I approach that as an actor. That is to say, "I dig into roles to harvest their souls." To find out what the fruit of that character could be, and to portray each one. In fact, I think that's why I write. I write because I'm an actor. The writer is assigned to give the actor something to do, to create songs for the actor. But it is the actor that's putting the whole thing to work.

Cal: Would you say that some of your songs are monologues set to music?

Oscar: Certainly. Many of them are that. Monologues set to music, sort of tone poems. I don't write generally, the way the market has come to expect you to write songs. But then, that's always changing.

Bob: You grew up in Chicago. What was Chicago like at the time when you were growing up?

Oscar: I was born in 1926. I was in elementary school during the Depression, and folks were having pretty hard times. My father is a professional man, he's an attorney, and he used to do legal work for groceries. I mean, it would be sort of a straight barter system; he'd do what had to be done for the shoe store man and we'd go around and get shoes.

That's how we'd get paid. Our family had to double up. We lived with my aunt, grandmother, and uncle, in a pretty small place. Everybody had to band together to get through the period. I grew up in a ghetto. I didn't know it was **the ghetto** then; it was just a neighborhood. It was across the street from a great big park. We had a lot of fun playing cops and robbers, baseball, and football out in the park, depending upon what the season was. There was a wonderful alley what we played in; it was really just an aley behind my house. It was wonderful, because we were the only kids who were in it (laughs), and it was a gas! A lot of things that I've written about come out that alley. I went to public elementary school, and got interested in girls about the time when you were supposed to, when nature told me. One thing about my childhood there was that they used to have the Regal Theatre. I used to see a lot of good shows for a dime, on Saturday. We could go over and see Duke Ellington, Count Basie, Cab Calloway, Fatha Hines; everybody was coming through there. And it was only a dime until you turned twelve, and I was so short that I stayed twelve for fourteen years (laughter). They finally said "Man, you've been coming here too long to still be payin' half fare" (laughs), and then it only went up to about a quarter. In those days that was a lot of money for a kid to get together. But as I said, for a dime you could see some of the best acts, man, some of the funniest comedians, like Dusty Fletcher, Patterson and Jackson, Buck and Bubbles, and Moms Mabley. All these people I saw as a kid.

Bob: Were you identifying with the stage at that time?

Oscar: I was just part of the audience. I used to be in a little theatre group when I was around Chicago. I always liked to act, but I didn't see myself projected particularly in that direction. I grew up with a family of lawyers; my father was a lawyer and a couple of uncles were also. That was the outlook that I had at that point.

Bob: When did that change?

Oscar: In college. After I went to high school, I went to the University of Wisconsin as a pre-law major. They assigned me to the regular pre-law curriculum, Botany, and Spanish, and man, I flunked out of school. I mean, I could not figure out why I had to conjugate Spanish verbs. I am fifty years old, and I have never at any point in my life ever had to say anything in Spanish. I knew **Si** and **no** (laugh) **nada** and a few things like that (laughter), **aqui**. But as far as absolutely having to, I've never had to and it used to be very difficult for me to sit down late, at night trying to get

together for a test in Spanish, when I figured, well man, if I went to Mexico, I would learn all this quick. You know "Where's the bathroom?''; "I'n hungry,'' (laughter), all that stuff. It would be necessity. But. . . .like with Botany, I'm crazy about the trees, but I'm not concerned about the tree's sex life. I don't want to get that deeply into trees. (laughs) I just want to get under them when they're shady.

Bob: So you weren't relating too much to that?

Oscar: No, and I didn't know why, you see. It was a source of some frustration, because the family pressures in general were for you to succeed in college and to go along with the program, and when you didn't the weight was on you to try to explain yourself, and you couldn't. I couldn't

Cal: Did you attend several different

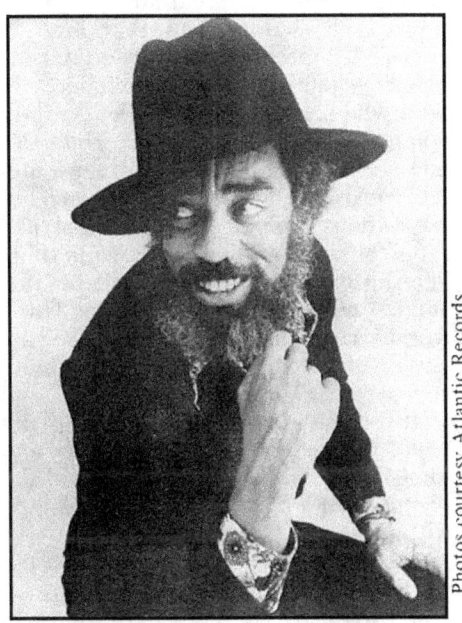

colleges?

Oscar: Yeah man, I went to like five different colleges.

Bob: All trying to pursue that. . . . academic thing.?

Oscar: Yeah, that academic thing, but I had switched from a pre-law major to an English major, because I wanted to write.

Bob: You were focusing now.

Oscar: That's right. At the University of Wisconsin, I flunked everything except English Composition. In English, if they wanted a 100-word theme, I'd write a 100-word poem, 'cause I was off into poetry then and that stuff, and I was studying. I'd go to the library and I'd read Keats, and Shelley; that's when I got acquainted with Countee Cullen and became familar with Langston Hughes and the kind of work that these men were doing. But I didn't know who I was or what I wanted to be. At Lincoln University I got cast in a play, and that

excited me, and then I flunked out. I had spoken to an aunt of mine whom I had met down in Baltimore, when I was at Lincoln University. She told my parents about how enthusiastic I was about the play. So when I flunked out of there and it came time to decide, "Well, where are we going to send the renegade this time?'' they sent me to Columbia College, which was a school for radio and T.V. communications. At that point I really started getting into the acting thing, and I stayed with that for quite a while. Let me back-track a minute. While I was in high school, I became a professional actor in radio. They used to have fifteen-minute programs for kids in the evening. They started around four o'clock. They would include programs like **Jack Armstrong**, **Lil Orphan Annie**, and **Don Winslow**, and **Tarzan of the Apes**, and the one that I was on was called, **The Secret City**. I did a six-week stint as one of the characters. That was my first job as a professional. So I've been a professional entertainer for about 35 years now. After I got out of Lincoln and went to Columbia, I began acting in radio quite steadily, working on shows written by a man by the name of Dick Durham, who just authored the book about Muhammed Ali. Dick's a marvelous writer and magnificent man who's had a great influence on my life. So, Dick was writing this show. . .and he was an excellent writer, and touchable. I could talk to him and he inspired me to aim for a certain quality of writing, although all good writers do. A guy asked me once, "How do I know that I can write?" and I said, "Because I can read." I've been reading good writing. I've been studying Shakespeare; I think that Richard Wright is dynamite; I think Dick Durham is dynamite, and having seen that, I have certain standards.

Bob: So you're your best critic?

Oscar: Well, maybe not my best critic, but my first critic. (laughter) I'm the one it starts with. I have to have some confidence in it in order for me to sit down and do it, because writing is a relatively lonely business, unless you're collaborating. Even then it's lonely with the 2 or 3 of you who are doing the collaboration. Generally, it's just one person in a room with a typewriter, or with a piece of paper and a pen.

Bob: Would you say that you're an isolationist or a loner? Is the process of writing easy for you?

Oscar: I used to like to **have written**, but I didn't like to **write**; that I found tedious and boring. As I've developed in it and been at it, I find that I now enjoy the process. I enjoy writing. I guess I am a loner to a certain extent. I feel a contradiction, in that, I am gregarious to a

Photos courtesy Atlantic Records

certain extent. I don't mind jumping up on stage and making a spectacle of myself, and I find it easy to be in front of people. I find it easy to be by myself. I can sit in a room like this one, or in a small hotel room, and if I'm working on a project, I don't need anybody. Eating gets to be a chore, an interruption. It takes me away from what I'm thinking about. But the most important time, to me, is that time when you start taking the thing off the printed page and putting it up on the stage. That is when you've conceived of a thing, you've had an idea; you're in the shower, or in the street, in a cab, and the germ of an idea hits you. It might be one character, and that kicks off the rest of them. That might be a long process, until you finally get that completed property, that finished script. It's all in place, and you've gone through the labor, and then you start production. You go into breathing the life into it, and that is sort of godly. That is the most exciting period, because you see this thing coming to life, you see it happening, and there are always problems. Great problems and headaches and things that won't work the way you thought they would work. Things that work better than you thought they would. And it's usually under some money pressure, 'cause you usually have to stay under a certain budget judiciously. You've got a prescribed time, in order to open on a specific date, and everything has got to go that way. Well, I get so involved during that period that I don't even lie down to give my clothes a rest (laughs). I'm so wrapped in it. I'm just going!!!

Bob: Would you say that you're more of a performer than a writer?

Oscar: It would be too strange for me to decide. It's just one person. The actor is stimulating the writer, but the writer likes to work, too, now and then. I enjoyed that artist-in-residence thing with young people.

Bob: What was that all about?

Oscar: Well, the one at Hunter College was something that we undertook which was under the SEEK program. Dr. Milton Martin hired Jean Pace and me to put together a program for young people who were involved in the SEEK program. He was the director. We thought we'd only be there for about six weeks. We wound up staying there for about six months. Largely because the college really couldn't find any facilities for us to rehearse. At the 68th street branch they really didn't have the facilities, (where we originally began the program) generally speaking, for the kind of show business that we were doing. But despite that, we were able to come up with a program called **Seek and Ye Shall Find.** That was a show that

involved, I guess, around 35 to 50 SEEK students; they had a band and dancers and singers and excellent entertainers. By mounting that show during the winter and spring semester, we were able to provide something that those young people worked out of all summer. That show appeared all over New York City, and they were remunerated for their performances. I felt very good about that. . . They needed a lot of working with. Generally speaking, when you find them in college, a lot of them have been sapped down. There's a joke I heard about. . .a teacher asked a student, "What is the difference between ignorance and apathy?" and the student said, "I don't know and I don't care." You find a great deal of that among young people; they don't understand English. . .now I'm really off into English. I mean, I work in the English language. I have a great admiration for it as such, but beyond that kind of specialized interest in it. . .it's the code in which the game is being operated. So, if you don't know the code, how are you going to know the game? You can't have any thoughts that you can't put into words! If you got a pool hall vocabulary, you're going to have a pool hall range of ideas. If all you can do is think in terms of legalisms, if you're a lawyer, you're not going to understand the world apart from that, perhaps. So that you're not doing the society a favor to cop the code in which the game, and your life, is being played. You're giving yourself some power to deal with it, and to be able to peep the whole card of the people that you're living around and with.

Cal: What was your experience in dealing with the Black Stone Rangers?

Oscar: Well, the Black Stone Rangers were a gang that had quite some notoriety in Chicago. They were accused of a great many things, murder, extortion and all kinds of things. . .they had a very bad image. And they lived up to some of it. So I went to talk to them. I asked them, "Why are you fighting each other. Why is black youth fighting one another? Do you perceive this to be the real problem?" And they said, "No", but they were in it now. . . trying to get a truce. There were vengeful people on both sides who'd been hurt or who have friends who'd been hurt or killed.

Bob: So the momentum had already been started?

Oscar: Yeah, so to get a truce was quite an operation. Then, the Chicago police department, after you'd get a truce, they'd let some mad dog out of jail who was not in on the truce, and he'd off somebody and then you'd have it all to do again. That was the big

problem with them. The problem with Black youth in general is to get them to perceive who they are and where they are. They think of themselves as immigrants. We are not immigrants. Black people were bought to this country for values that are intrinsic; the value was in the black person. We didn't come here seeking our fortune or escaping oppression; we had freedom. So our whole thrust in America has been towards freedom, towards a return to what we had. Those folks from Europe came here to escape from slavery, trying to find freedom. So they had a different psyche that they brought in in the first place. They were prepared to listen to a bunch of jive; they were prepared to live with Nixon. Nixon got the greatest landslide, and was the biggest crook they ever had. They were cool about that. I heard one guy on some T.V. analysis program say that he predicted that Nixon's biggest problem after his landslide election would be race relations. Well, it was, because it was a Black man that pulled the tape off (laughter) and exposed Watergate (Frank Wills). It just came at him at a somewhat lower level than they had anticipated, but it's all there. I'm not afraid of white people anymore. I used to be, because they were mean and they'd kill ya. When I grew up they were lynching Black folks in the South all the time. I knew what that meant and my father was always a very militant man in somewhat orthodox ways; he was never the kook that I am. He was always stable and right-on and did not accept white racism at all! Ever! He was advocating a 49th state; so I knew what was going on as a kid. He wanted to get Black folks together in the '30's. So I grew up in this kind of atmosphere. My parents are really wonderful. I'm a monument to redemptive love. I mean, I was doin' stuff that they didn't know what the hell I was doing, and I wouldn't explain it, but they just kept giving me other chances. . .up to this day. They've been married fifty years now, and that support was very helpful. I felt that there was a lot of things that I had. . .cause you gotta have help, there are a lot of things that I had then. I have to pass it on; I'm a relay racer. It's not just a solo operation here. I don't ever expect to arrive at a point where I can say, "And we lived happily ever after." So in dealing with Black young people you got to try to put them in the process of the relay race. Wake up, take the baton and run.

Bob: In some cases they can't conceptualize what the entire game is about.

Oscar: That's right.

Bob: So therefore they can't see their

part in it.

Oscar: First of all, evidently, the school system does not equip them to cope with the game as it's being played.

Bob: How much responsibility do you think that parents have in the educational process? How much should happen in the home?

Oscar: I don't know. Of course, they're always blaming it on the parents. The parents blame the schools, the schools blame the parents. I would imagine that somehow it would have to be some reciprocal thing that's worked out. I don't really have answers to all these things. I have a whole bunch of questions. I think that sometimes the questions are important. For instance, if I'm in a car with a druken driver, my first responsibility is to stop the car. I don't have to have a driver's license or a road map. **My first responsibility** is to stop the car. Now we'll discuss who's going to drive and where we're going and all that. But first let's stop doing the dumb thing, the suicidal thing. Of course, it's not required that any one person have all the answers. We are all going to have to figure this thing out. We're going to have to arrive at certain realizations, like the driver is drunk. In the situation in this country, now, the driver is definitely drunk, stoned out of his skull and talking nonsense.

Cal: Considering the history of minorities in this country, how do you relate to the Bicentennial and its treatment in the media?

Oscar: I don't know how to respond to that as far as what they're going to do with that. Whatever, it'll be like a commercial on TV. It won't have any deep abiding effect because. . .what are black people going to do about the Bicentennial? Are they going to celebrate their participation in the freedom of America? Because we have been America's greatest fighters for freedom. Irregardless of whether or not we got paid, whether or not we got it in our hand, we have pushed it in that direction. Our music, our dance, is worth more than all the cotton ever picked, all the tobacco ever planted. We have given America more than it could ever have stolen from us, free. What would they be doing, what would they be dancing, what would they be singing, would music be? They'd still be square dancing! We have given that. We should celebrate ourselves. We should understand what we've done and what we have. We are the most communicative people in the world, the most entertaining people in the world. Demonstratively so! The Beatles come back and proved it; they take our music and make 17 million dollars in 6 months. Is that making enough money for you?

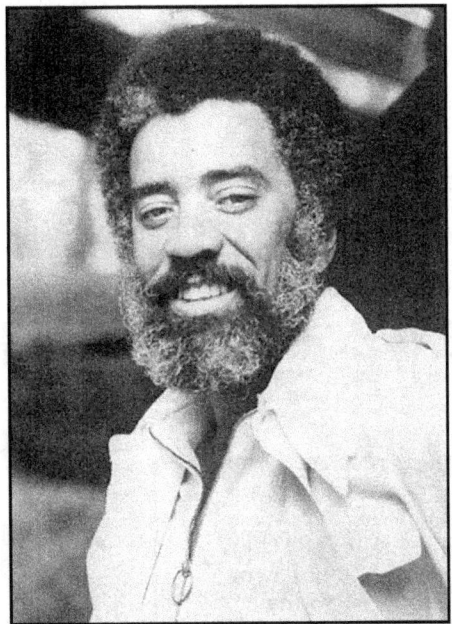

Bob: What is the relationship of music as it relates to our culture?

Oscar: Well, let me first start by telling you what I think culture is. Culture is the sum of your experiences. What you've been through and how you express that in painting, poetry, playwriting or however. That is your culture. I think that this is the other thing that unifies Black people; it is our common culture. In addition to our common oppression, we have a common culture. One time, I was performing in San Fransisco and some young people came to one of our concerts. . . came from all over the country, about 4 or 500 of 'em. At the end of the show we invited the audience to come up on the stage and dance. Well, our audience that night just filled the stage; every corner of the stage was just filled with young Black teenagers dancing. They were all dancing "the popcorn." Whether they were from Texas or N.Y., Illinois or California, they were all doing that same thing. So we have that, too, in common. The presentation of the human image artistically is the highest thing that can happen. Art, then, as it comes out of the culture in the form of painting, in the form of dance helps people to draw conclusions from life. You get the Art of Living. I see our need to have a cultural revolution in which we get to put our own terms on the air, on the stage. Slaves were not allowed theatre because the dramatic conclusions that the slave would draw up from his experiences would contradict, or certainly conflict, with the interest of the master. So the master sees to it that you don't have any theatre, perceiving that you can see then that the theater is a liberating force. It would change the image that is being projected. What would it do? It would attract money and power and influence to the ones who are doing the projecting, to the forces doing the projecting. If we had our own theatre, we would have a means for building our own Disneylands, and our own Lincoln Centers, and all of the ancillary things that vent off that; the cleaning shops that are going to clean the costumes, the seamstress that's going to sew them, and the painters that are going to do that, and the construction people who are going to put up our buildings. We could do that out of our own culture, out of our own talent. That was what that Blackstone Ranger thing was aimed at doing, to give these young Black kids an alternative. You don't have to go over here and knock this off, and rip that off. Why don't you organize what you are, put that in a beautiful form and sell tickets! When we did that, nobody's going to snatch the purse of the old lady who's coming in voluntarily to pay for a three-dollar ticket, stand up and give you a great ovation, and go out and tell her friends and neighbors to come over with their three dollars. That cools out the whole thing. If you want the have-nots to act like the haves, give them something. Soon as someone has something to conserve, they become a conservative. With nothing to conserve you are definitely out there.

Cal: Do you think that an actor on television has a different effect on audiences than an actor in the theater?

Oscar: That tends to depend upon the talent of the actor, on the skill of the production. I saw Red Foxx do a *Sanford and Son* show live in the studio in Burbank. Sitting there is like sitting in a theatre. They were as good seeing them there in the flesh as when I saw that program on TV. It wasn't that much different as far as the quality of the performance, there is no difference, It's the same thing being pictured another way. Motion pictures should be brought into this too because that's also a heavy influence on people's lives. What if Black people had our own motion picture industry? Their own theatres? They'd only have to have about 50 across the country. One or two studios to put out your movies, your own images. Put out your own movies, discuss your own history, criticize yourselves. Have all those things that go on now, but you've got to do it yourself, too. You've got to be your own representatives and advocates. You can't expect the man who's enslaving you to cut you loose; he didn't bring you over here to cut you loose!

Bob: Since you've had 35 years experience in the field of entertainment, what things do you think that young actors or actresses should address themselves to? *Cont'd on page 54*

Woodie King, Jr. Directs "The Long Night"

Woodie King, Jr. is one of the leading theatrical producers in this country. His most recent successes are Ed Bullins' The Taking of Miss Janie (which received the New York Drama Critics Circle Award) and the Obie Award-winning drama The First Breeze of Summer, by Leslie Lee. King produced Ron Milner's popular play What The Wine-Sellers Buy, which has played to packed houses both on Broadway and across the country. Currently, he is producing Medal of Honor Rag at the Theater De Lys.

Triumphant in his endeavors up to the present, Woodie King, Jr. is receiving new acclaim as a film director. His soon-to-be-released film, The Long Night was chosen as the American entry at this year's "New Directors/New Films" festival at Lincoln Center.

Based upon a short story by Julian Mayfield, The Long Night was co-produced by Woodie King, Jr. and St. Clair Bourne (who directed the highly respected film Let The Church Say Amen). Mayfield and King collaborated on the screenplay.

Impressions asked Woodie King, Jr. to talk about the experience of producing The Long Night independently and his plans for distributing the film:

Raising the funds to produce *The Long Night* basically involved the preparation of a portfolio, and getting the information out to those people who could afford to invest. There were many people who worked on the project without receiving salaries, because they felt that the film was an important venture. They understand that they will be paid once the film is distributed. We cannot distribute the film unless a certain amount of money comes in to pay off bills. Getting a distributor is just a matter of showing it around, and my belief is that if you have a good project, you can get a distributor. Of course, this is dependent upon whether you want to go for the deals which they want you to arrange. Personally, I feel that even if I don't find a distributor, I have no problems with the idea of opening the film myself in maybe eight of nine cities.

What prompted you to make The Long Night *into a film?*

I liked the story, which is basically concerned with the Black family structure, and one family coming together. The film depicts the breaking up of a family due to external pressure. The father is placed in a situation which motivates him to abandon his family. I tried to show how they had to exist with the strongest piece of the link missing, and through the use of flashbacks,

how strong the family was when all its members were together. The film is concerned with the family's struggle to overcome all of those obstacles that are out there for Black people.

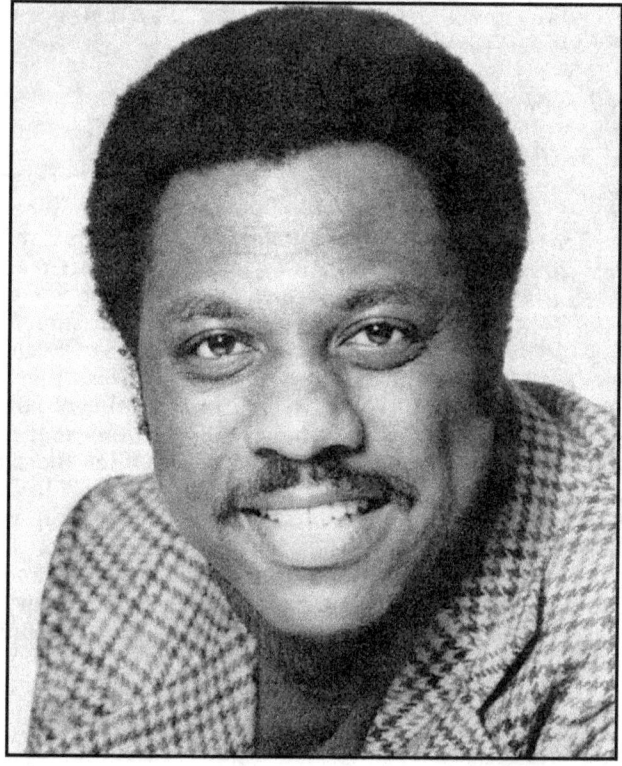

Why is it that, after a certain point in the film, the mother never appears again?

Because it was not about the mother. It was about the *family*; it is not about any one of those people. And since the young kid (played by W. Geoffrey King) is faced with making decisions which are crucial to his future direction, we can clearly see the test of his upbringing through his actions. In order to become a man, he must overcome those same forces that his father has had to overcome. He must either do that or become that mysterious old man who digs in garbage cans, the character of which serves as an important metaphor in the film.

Was the old man meant to exist on a mythological level?

Yes. He represents a mythological fear of the unknown. We cringe when we see Bowery bums; we cringe when we see derelicts of our society. There is a reluctance on our part to acknowledge the existence of such people, but we don't want to do anyting to stop others from going in that direction. We have to act to stop that. When we see that a young person might be going in that direction, we have to take the responsibility of showing him a better way to deal with his life.

There was an ornament at the top of the old man's

stick. Was that the African symbol of life?

Right. It represents fertility. If you watched very closely, you would notice that before the old man would dig in the garbage, he would sprinkle powder on his hand. This is because, in those things that have to be cast away, there are good things as well as bad things. And the chant that the old man was singing was a Haitian chant. He was saying, "Sunflowers, children, people should save their children." The rhythm of the chant, I feel, is more important than the actual words, so in terms of understanding the significance of the chant, I feel it doesn't really matter that it's in Haitian dialect. The fact that the boy can't understand the old man, and more or less avoids him, illustrates the sense of aversion that some children have for older people. I feel that this is tragic, because children could learn so much from older people if their parents instilled in them a certain understanding of their elders. But we know that as children grow older, their understanding of their elders does grow accordingly.

How do you see the future of independent film-making in this country?

I think it's the only way to go. I think that, as more Black people become aware that making a film is like any other form of art, they will begin to move toward it more and more. It doesn't have to be as expensive as the papers would have us believe. We can make good art films. I see *The Long Night* as an urban *Sounder*, if you will. *The Long Night* is similar to the post-war neo-realistic films. I wanted to deal with showing certain styles of architecture in Harlem. I wanted to bring out the smallness of the boy against huge backgrounds. The City College campus provided a good location for some of the shooting. I used streets to point out that, at certain times of the day, such as mid-afternoon, there is no one on the streets. When the boy was going to get the money from the numbers lady, he went maybe two blocks and there was nobody on the street. And I didn't

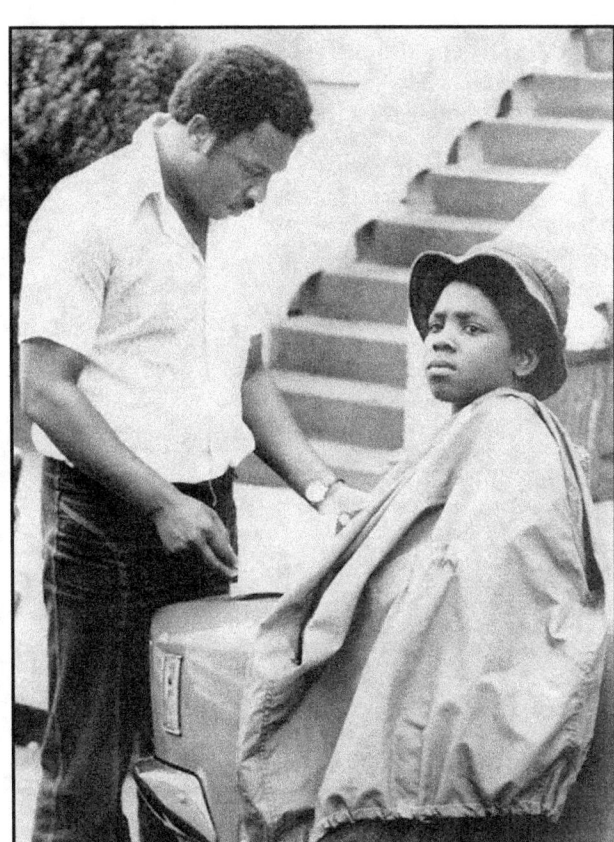

Woody King, Jr. directing *The Long Night* with his son, W. Geoffrey King.

Photo by Bert Andrews

have to set that up. But then he moves into another section of the street and it's readily apparent that the streets are full. When the mother, father and son are walking in the street, there is a contrast between them and the old age homes which they are walking past, where people are slowly disintegrating. Here, I think, we see what the family really has to face: will one's life here for this really short span of time, be of value, or will it have been for nothing? Those are the kinds of questions which I feel that films should try to answer. Films have to be planned carefully in order to reach a quality of filmmaking that will last forever. The script must strive to embody such qualities. A film is forever! My hope is that your great-grandchildren will be able to view *The Long Night* and get a good idea of what life was like in 1975. That this is the way that certain things looked, and that is the way that certain people reacted, and the way they talked.

What kind of influence do the major film companies exert over movie theater owners? Do the major companies discourage theaters from picking up independent films?

If you present the theaters with a film that will make them money, they will buy it from you. If my whole existence depended upon whether one of the seven major distribution companies wanted to pick up my film, I would be in a sad situation, and in that case I shouldn't have made the film in the first place. When I made the film, I knew that if it wasn't picked up by one of the major distributors, I could distribute it myself. I don't have any problems with opening the film in Detroit, Atlanta, Cleveland or Oakland. If Black people come out to see it and like it, it will be a hit; if they don't like it, it will only show me that I made a mistake. In that case, I would put it on the shelf. Then maybe I'd bring it out again ten years from now, and ask them again if they like it. ✿ —**C.W.**

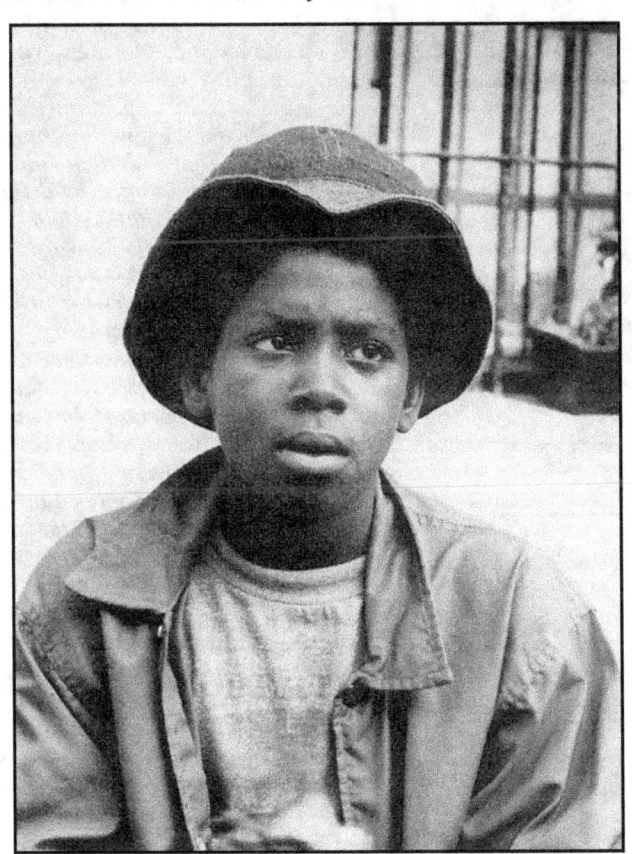

W. Geoffrey King in *The Long Night.*

Photo by Bert Andrews

FROM "SWEETBACK"

MELVIN VAN PEEBLES

TO "THE TRUE AMERICAN"

Of the many speeches that I had to give in my college English class, this was the one that I really enjoyed. Basically, the assignment involved talking about somebody, in the news or in my life, whom I felt personified a particular quality that I respected. The moment I heard the assignment it took little time for me to visualize the person and the quality that I was going to talk about in my upcoming speech.

The person was Melvin Van Peebles, and the quality was the "will to succeed." "The Will To Succeed" was a concept that had fascinated me for a long time. I often pondered the reasons why some people rose to heights, able to actualize themselves, while others seemed to opt for mediocrity. For as Oscar Brown, Jr. has stated, "It takes just about as much energy or more to be mediocre as it does to be excellent."

The speech, I was told in the class critique was filled with enthusiasm, as my obvious affinity to my subject matter helped make my delivery convincing and powerful. After the class was over, many of my classmates posed questions to me concerning Melvin Van Peebles' career as well as asking about this dubious concept called the "will to succeed." Dealing with the concept at that time gave me an opportunity to share some positive ideas with others about the potential that I feel is inherent in each of us. Explaining, I said that each of us is unique and that it is our personal responsibility to strive towards discovering our uniqueness and to seek to provide ourselves with the proper soil and nourishment necessary for our creative growth. It was necessary to point out that the desire for that exploration is very important, but it is also important that we develop the tenacity to hang in there when things get difficult and the way becomes blurred. As novelist John Oliver Killens puts it, "We have to learn to be Long Distance Runners." (See Impressions Magazine. Vol. 1 #3)

Some years have pased since that speech, yet the essential kernel of my belief has remained intact, and my respect for the integrity of Melvin Van Peebles' accomplishments and energy has increased as he continues to move forward on any number of levels pratically simultaneously.

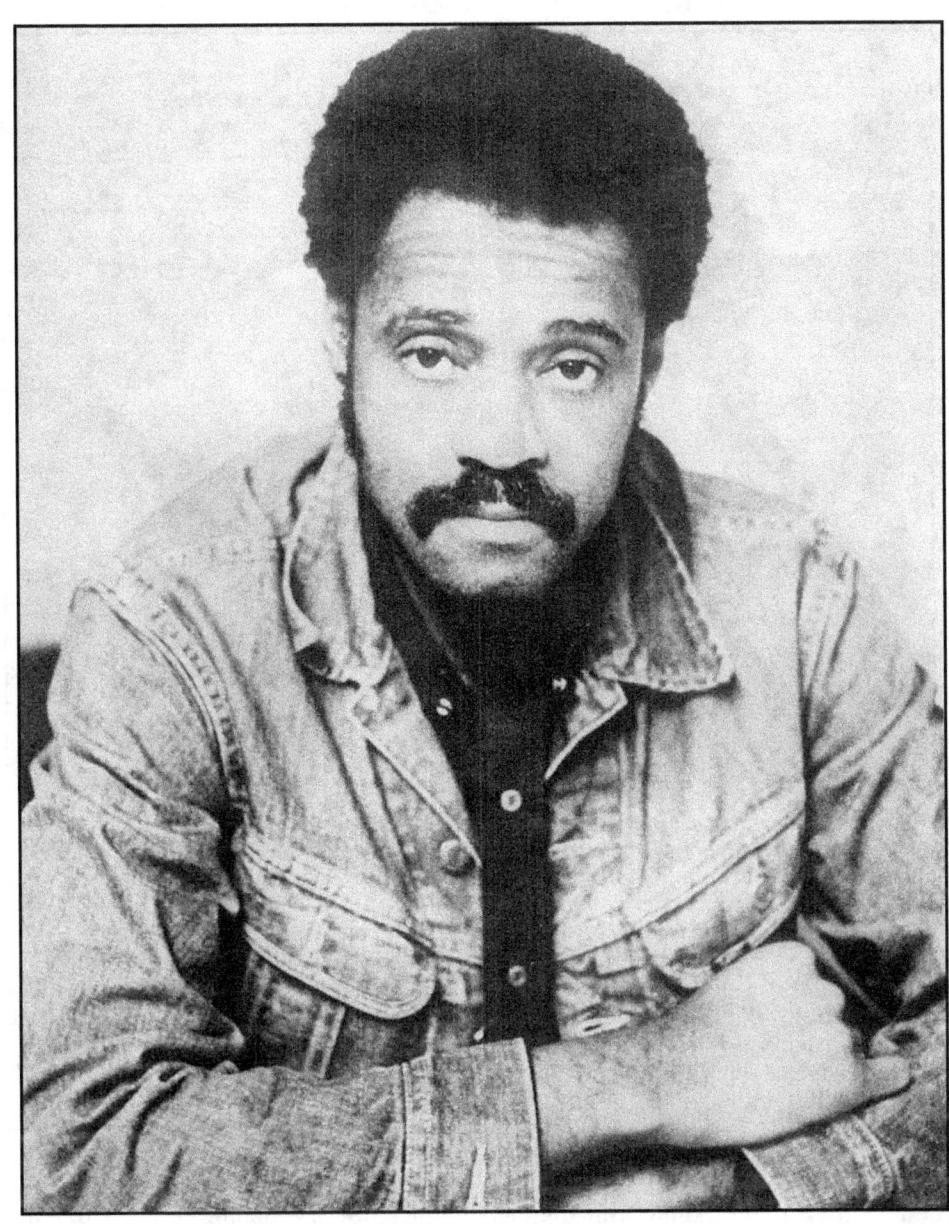

In this first exclusive interview since the release of his hilarious new novel, The True American, published by Doubleday, Melvin talks with us about his ideas concerning art, including his approach to art, providing insights into the witty and pragmatic world in which he lives. He first received national attention as the French delegate to the San Francisco International Film Festival with the presentation of his film, The Story of a Three Day Pass. After returning to Hollywood, Melvin directed the highly successful movie Watermelon Man, which starred Godfrey Cambridge. Being independent by nature (and choice) Melvin scored, wrote, produced, directed, starred in and distributed (whewww!) the historic SWEET SWEETBACK'S BAADASSSSS SONG, which is one of the largest-grossing films in the history of the motion picture industry. Moving to the theatre, his play Ain't Supposed To Die A Natural Death, on Broadway, was viewed by critics and audiences alike as a landmark achievement and received a Tony nomination for best musical. A gifted singer-composer, Melvin's most recent album, What the. . . .You Mean I Can't Sing? (on the Atlantic Label) was a popular success. His other recordings, on the A&M label, include Brer Soul and Ain't Supposed To Die A Natural Death. In addition to his new novel The True American, Melvin has penned such books as The Big Heart and A Bear For The F.B.I. He made Broadway history as the first producer to have two musicals, Ain't Supposed To Die A Natural Death and Don't Play Us Cheap, running concurrently. Recently, Melvin co-hosted Black Journal on WNET.

The following interview with Melvin gave us (Cal Wilson and myself) a first-hand opportunity to inquire into his motivations and hopefully answer some of the many questions that have been floating around concerning the mythology of Melvin Van Peebles.

Cal Wilson: It's been said that one of the problems that filmmakers have is that they fail to use the visual element to it's full capacity. How much do you consider yourself a photographer in terms of your film technique?

Melvin Van Peebles: Hmm. It's all quite an integral part of the way I work. As you know, I basically moved into cinema because I'm a writer. Well. . . that's even a hedge. . . Let me put it this way, for years I used to laugh when I looked back on my early childhood. I was raised to be a minister. This is when I was about ten or fourteen years old, that is what my mother wanted me to be, a minister. I laughed at what a funny idea that was, until I realized, maybe something happened unconsciously, but I am preaching. I really don't concern myself with the visual per se, or the audio per se or the. . .I have something that I want to say, and I never thought about it. I guess the visual is very important, but I don't think of it as a separate entity from all of the rest of what I'm trying to say. Do you follow me? I writing a new novel now, and I've written the story as a play already, which I haven't yet put on. When I take it from a play to a novel, there's a whole change. There's a change because a novel is one step further along in its final form when it gets to the reader, whereas a play is for the eyes outside of the dialogue, the eyes of the director and the actors who then take it to its final form. When I do a movie, I think of the visual probably as the final form that I would be taking it to if I were doing a novel. As to what style is, it's the way you do something, the way you think. You can probably consciously acquire a style, or you can just do it as it comes to you. Correcting, of course, for intelligibility, for the speed with which your mind works, the speed of the typewriter and the personalities of a number of lecturers, readers who you've never met, or viewers who you've never seen. I went into movies, as I went into all the other things. Let me begin the odyssey of how I went into these things. I used to be a painter, so I guess the visual is very important. I lived in Mexico. I had scholarships as a painter. I didn't know many black people, who were into painting, who affected very strongly their immediate lives. I wanted to affect our immediate lives. So from there I went into books, because I felt I could reach a broader audience, and books are beginning now to affect our lives. At the time they weren't affecting our lives that much on a one to one basis, and I looked around and said, where was the large effect being made on our lives, or where are our images of ourselves being formed, and one place, I felt, was in the theatre. That would be about the third place down on the ring; after that would come television and movies, and if television and movies was where it was happening, where I could find a platform. . .this is where I go back to that minister that I thought that I had quit as a child. That's where I could talk to the folks, so that's where I went. When I went there, I didn't go with the thought of style. I didn't know the difference between 16mm and 35mm. I knew how stuff looked; I didn't realize the a priori supposition that I was making of a subjective judgement. I was just doin' it. Like someone may thing that he's just playing the horn, but he's heard Bird, he's hip to Cecil's [Taylor] chords, just by the fact of him being out there of this time. And if he's not hip to Cecil's chords, some guy who we heard who stole it from Cecil, he's hip to it.. . . So I don't know! I have to caution you that in an interview with myself, I won't pontificate, cause I don't know that much about it. I went to movies 'cause I was sittin' in a movie one night and said, "Shit, I could do better than that." I just got tired of seeing what I was seeing. . . When I said that, I was not talking about the lighting, I was not talking about the action, the pace, the montage. I didn't even know that those things even existed. They were just there! I knew I got tired of seeing niggas humming spirituals everytime they were getting lynched. And that was my point of view, where I attacked from, and where I went to, and that was the construction and the idea which I had that launched me into the arts, onto movies. Of course, everybody said that I was crazy. My cinematic education consisted of a guy I know showing me how to

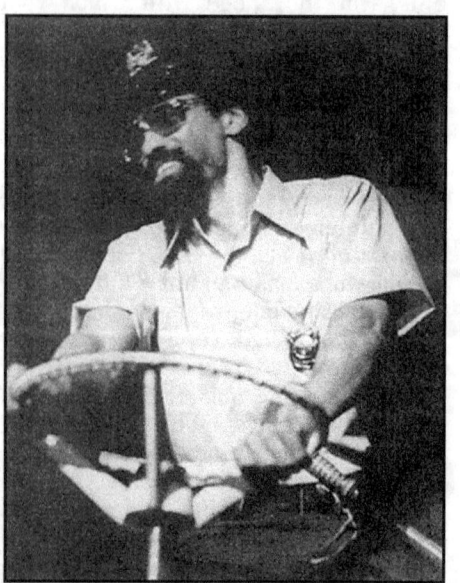

Dick A. Williams in *Ain't Suppose To Die A Natural Death.*

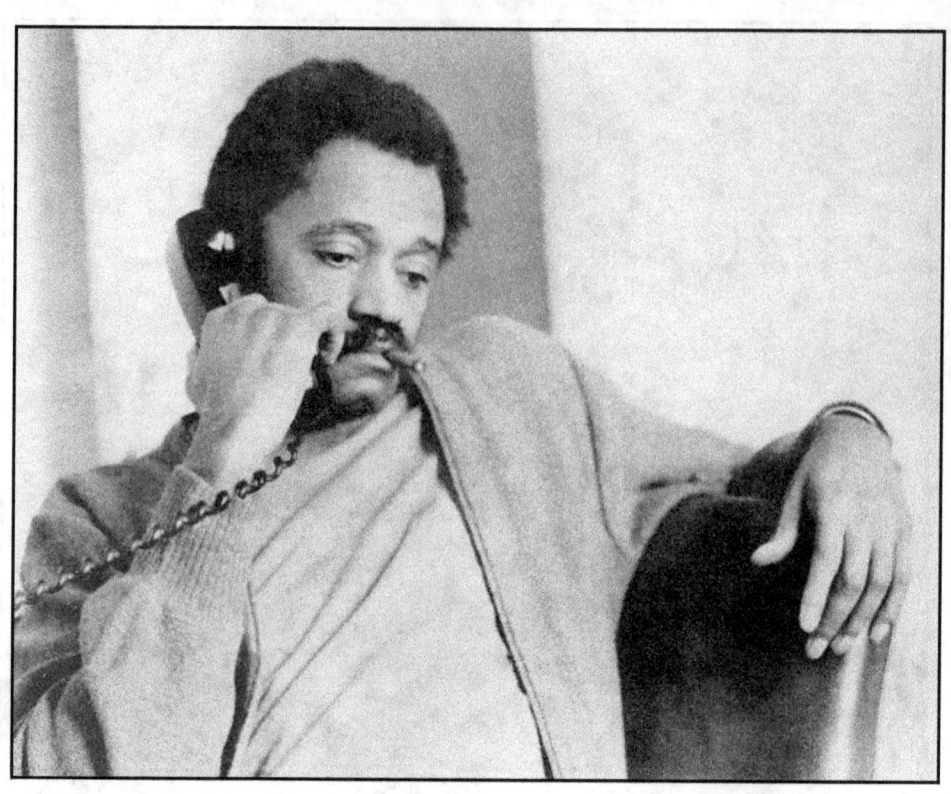

Photo by Bob Bryan

splice two pieces of film together. That's all anybody ever taught me. I didn't know that that was called montage yet, and the first time I went into a studio, a cat says "What did you do?", and I said, well, I did this, and he said, "You don't do all those things." I didn't know that. Hey, I didn't know, 'cause I had nobody to show me. Not knowing what I didn't know, I just went right ahead and did it. You dig where I'm coming from? And people have talked about my style, or the lack of it, or how defined it is. I don't know! But the fact is that each one of us has a creative finferprint, and that creative fingerprint by lesser people, then gets diluted. See, everyone is trying to put life into a manageable rule of thumb, because it is such an unruly, hurly-burly, bubbling, whirling thing. And if we can construct rules. . .and there are possibilities of finding lines of comprehension in works, but, myself, I don't bother with the lines of the work. I do the work and let somebody else find the lines. Now a lot of times people. . .there are two kinds of critics. There are the brilliant perceptive critics, those who agree with me, (laughter) and then there's them ignorant mothafucka's who don't (laugh) and I don't even bother about them. You know where I'm coming from, and that's just where Im at.

Bob Bryan: Understanding that the ideas that you are projecting, do you consciously think about the style in which you construct a piece of work?

Melvin: Well, I do think about style,

but I don't know if it's called style. It's like when you see a chick and you want to hit on her, "now how an I goin' to get her." You are talking about style. Now, you may not call it style. . .I remember a buddy and I were at a thing, and there was this girl, and we wanted to hit on her. O.K.? So we flipped a coin, and I won. So I was a rough cat, so I said, "Hey baby, you gonna give me some?" (laughter) She said (affected), "no". He was standing in the corner, his shot. "Hi, how long you been here, you want some coffee?" Boom, he copped. That was it! Now, if he would have done my thing, I would have copped. She might have said, "Hey, I'm down for the git-down," then he would have been out. But from a more analytical person, in a distant way, looking at, "Well, you choose a style that. . ."Hey, I'm just trying to get over. . .when I tell a story, I'm just trying to tell it. For example, when I was doin' *Sweetback,* I wanted it to look all arm pits and elbows, man. I didn't want that smooth facade, and I worked. . .many times, I would take the film through a couple of generations to give it that rrrrr, you know, that glare that. . .like you use dissonance on a piano, 'cause you want to hear a thing and you don't know. . . I can't read or write music. I'd be just doin' a thing and a trained musician would say "Oh! that's G to a minus. . ." That's very interesting; I don't know what all that was, but I do know what made my left ear twitch good and my right shoulder feel well when I hit a certain thing, and

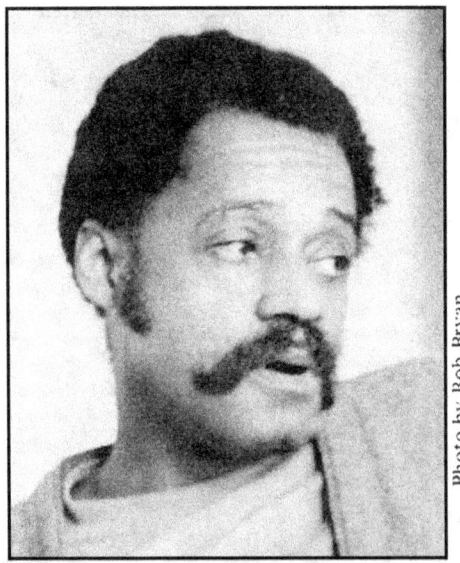

Photo by Bob Bryan

that's what I would do.

Bob: That's interesting because I think that a lot of people in this society don't do what they want to do because they are told that you have to be this or you have to be that; or that you have to specialize; or they get hung up on the terms instead of the feeling.

Melvin: Right. Well, now, I cannot claim intelligence for the things I did. I mean, I tried the other thing, but everytime I would try the other way, I would fart or I'd slip and I finally said, "Hey, man, you got to go with your style, you just got to go with the way you are." I mean, if I would try to enunciate correctly to somebody, I wouldendup cracking up, and so forth. Not having good sense, I had at least the street knowledge not to try and be something that I wasn't. I mean, I tried. No, since I've tried unsuccessfully to be something I wasn't, one day I said, "Well, fuck it!" You dig it! And from then on all blessings flew.

Bob: They've called you everything from genius, to whatever. How do you respond to being called these things?

Melvin: You mean, there are two people who call me these things—the ones who spell my name right and the ones who don't. "Early to bed, early to rise, work like hell and advertise." I don't mind. Look, ain't nobody called me nothin' when I was in the post office. Huh, Cat didn't even know my name; I

was just a number. He's already on my turf, if he bothers to call my name, to call me a whole bad thing.

Bob: When you reflexively look back at the ideas that you've put out in your books, in the theatre, and in movies, do you think that the things which really have changed people, or transformed them on some level happen because of the conscious consciousness or on a subconscious level?

Melvin: I think they can happen on a number of levels. Guys ask me how I felt about film or about theatre, and what I'm trying to do in the book. I went out to Hollywood when a nigga couldn't get arrested out there, huh. They got blacks in them unions now, blacks are doin' it all over, blacks are doin' it. Well, I like to think in a large part that I'm responsible for that. Even though sometimes I disagree with what they do. At least we're learning the craft, which allows, then, for people to interpolate and I think this was happening. I think it began to happen once they acquired the craft and had the opportunity. A lot of times young people come up to me and say, "Brother man, I want to do like you did," this and that and the other. I say, well, slow your roll. I spent ten years gettin' it together. I worked for the man, and so forth and so on, and scratched my head, and I shuffled this, that and the other, gettin' that thang. So we've managed to short-circuit that for you to some extent. Don't be intimidated and feel that I sprang full-blown with all of this knowledge. I learned it the hard

way, and a way that was harder than it had to be, or should be. But still, acquire the knowledge and don't be intimidated by it.

Bob: Then you're not intimidated by the mythology of Melvin Van Peebles?

Melvin: No! It don't bother me. You see, I decided you can be black-mailed by failure or white-mailed, whatever you want to call it. You can be intimidated by failure but you can also be intimidated by success, but me, I got laid before, so I ain't got nowhere to go.

Cal: You said that you were tired of seeing the kinds of things that black people were doing in the movies. . .

Melvin: No, I didn't. I said some of those things I might not like.

Cal: Yeah, some of those things you might not like. So, in essence, did you think that these acts in the films re-inforced behavior of people? What was it exactly that you didn't like about these things?

Melvin: Let's take, for example, the use of the establishment of force to steal control. . .I think that revolutionary films or the revolutionary aspects that I tried to show in **Sweetback**, for example, have been pre-empted and made counter-revolutionary, because now, any time a guy in the films kicks somebody elses ass, and we begin to yell for the hero, he pulls out a badge, or he pulls out a license. In other words, he's still, if you think about it, he's still working under daddy, huh; still working under daddy. Man, I saw a film—this chick came out and, bam, shot 95 million cats. Boom. I said Dy-no-mite. And police say, "Hey", then run up to her. She says, "Get away from me, mothafucka" and pulls out a badge. "Well, see, actually I'm an FBI agent. I work for the such and such," which reinforces in the mind of the audience, "Yes, he is still father", which is, as far as I'm concerned, hey, but that's a. . .I

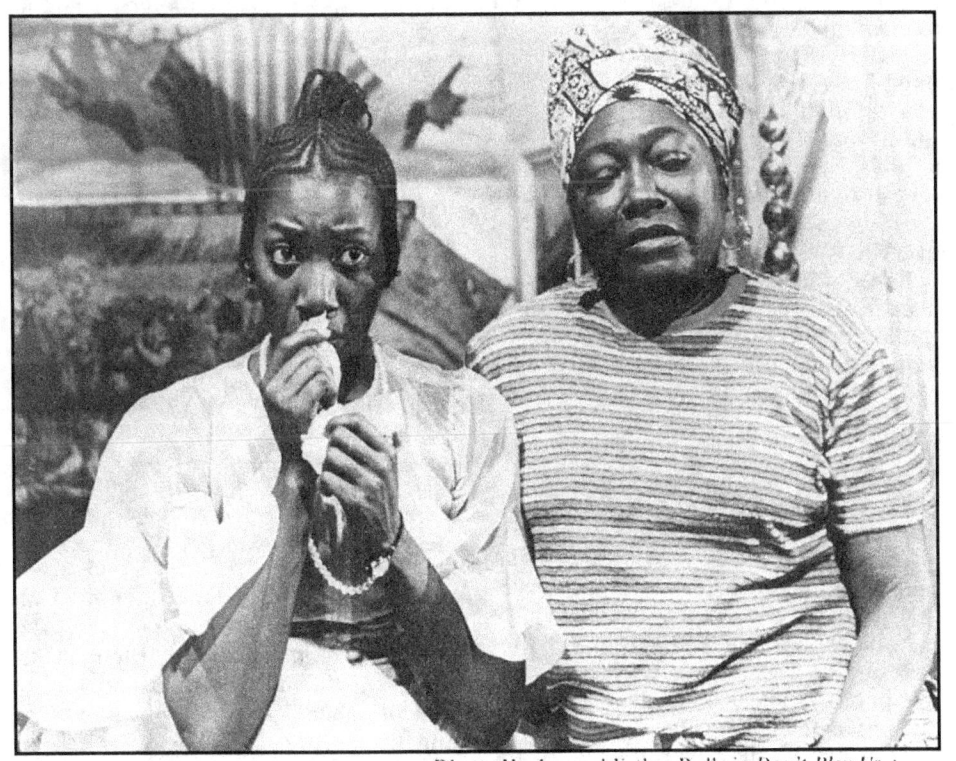

Rhetta Hughes and Esther Rolle in *Don't Play Us Is Cheap.*

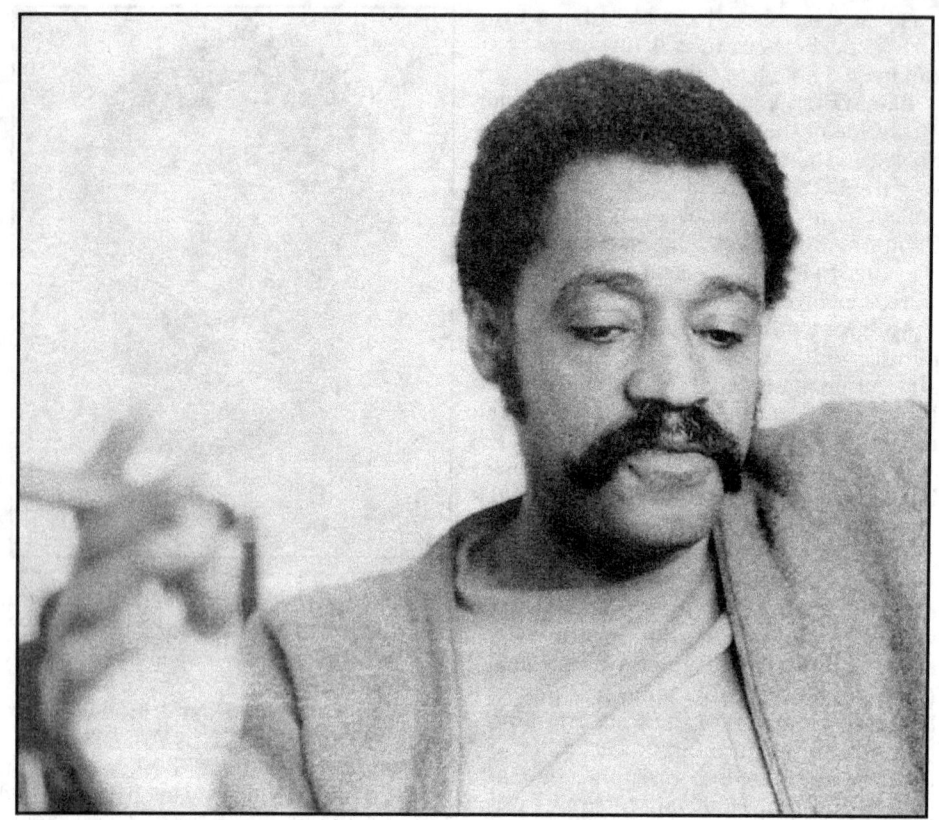
Photo by Bob Bryan

don't really deal with that.

Bob: There are a lot things, in your past, particularly, that you don't like to talk about, so I've heard.

Melvin: That's correct.

Bob: Why is that. . .without talking about the past?

Melvin: Because, when you haven't made it, or when you're just another nigguh, as soon as you do, they try and take episodes or reasons from you to diferientiate you from the other. "Oh, you were born in Chicago, that's why; all brilliant people come from Chicago." Well, there are black people down in Missouri who don't need to be intimidated about where somebody came from, you understand me? "Oh, you went to such and such a school, that's why it is you are so forth." They use that as a subtle differentiation. You see, once you've made it, the next move, if they can't keep you down, is to separate you, and this is part of this whole. . .like . . .sometimes people get very insulted, because I won't sign autographs. 'Cause it's not about that. It's not about me being. . .and I've seen a whole lot of cats turn left, man. You get up there, you were dynamite from the gitty-up, but then, as things went on, you kept signing those autographs and you kept saying (affects voice), "Well, yes, what do you think about such and such?" You start believing that shit. Now, I'm just as weak as the next person; the only way that I know, with the weaknesses that I have, is to avoid it. Just stay out of it, then I don't have to

get used to it. If I were king, my first decree, if I were king of the united states would be to take all of the fans out of the toilet, 'cause there are too many big-timers who don't think that their shit stinks, and let them once more realize that their shit stinks. . .

Bob: If you had the platform to ren un-crate your past, coming from **your** mouth, what would you say is important to mention?

Melvin: Coming from my mouth? It only takes two words. "I'm Black". If you count the apostrophe, that makes three words. That's all! Because all the rest. . .I mean, look I. . .I could leave the swankiest party, this, that and so forth. I can't get no cab any faster than everybody else.

Cal: For large periods of time, you've been outside of the country. Do you feel that a person, in order to really understand the American mentality, has to have spent time outside the country?

Melvin: It depends on the person. I didn't change. . .when I looked around to get the game together, to run the game I wanted to run, I had to woodshed. I had to have a place where the people weren't hip to what I was getting ready to put down. Now, don't forget that when I went down to Hollywood in '57, and said, hey, I'd like to get into film and so forth, I wrote a book that was published here ten years later, but I had published it elsewhere. People said, "Well, naw", they weren't ready for that. That's cool, that's cool 'cause once you understand that, then you have to go where you can go, and ho

you can go, and succeed by any means necessary. And succeeding by any means necessary at this time meant running to the left to hit to the right. Now, when the whole thing started was when I came back as a French delegate to the San Francisco Film Festival. Now, that put a hurtin' on the establishment, that was saying, "Well, one of these days we're going to let you in, when we think that those black fingers can manipulate our equipment. . .it's very complicated and your minds are still to close to the jungle, blah, blah", and all that other shit, you dig it. You've got to run, how where you can run. It's like asking a cat, well, why did you throw a pass instead of running? You look at which way your defense is lined up, and that's the way you make your move.

Cal: Now, I've heard you say that you plan to put out your ideas in as many forms of media as possible. When you came out with your record album, that was another way of dealing with people. Do you plan to go into radio or television, and what do you think would be the dynamic of your becoming involved in those fields?

Melvin: Well, its a time limitation of whatever I go into. You have to juggle your priorities. However, after *Sweetback*, I was able to borrow money and bogard money beforehand, because I promised everybody two for one. That is, I promised them that they could help me and feel liberal and that if I failed, then their racist theories would be vindicated. When I didn't fit their magnificence, or whatever that word is, to do another job, I would be SOL, but by having diversified. . .like any other corporation, that's why people diversify, because if nothing doesn't go here, you can be going somewhere else. You dig where I'm coming from? Just like, you be talking to a chick, and you see that one ain't gettin' over, so you switch. I'm just trying to get the man's foot out of my ass. My ass, if you have any social consciousness or understanding, you have to realize that in order to get him out of my ass, I have to get him out of your ass, too. So we've all got to work together. We've got to all work together, or I can put on the blinders of the middle class and say, well, as long as I got my little thing, then I'm safe. And I can have a limousine waiting for me, so that I can forget how hard and how much trouble it is to pick up a cab or walk. I take the subway now, I be sitting on the subway and people be looking at me, and they shake their heads, "You know, that cat looks like Melvin Van Peebles." "That couldn't be him. . ."

Bob: He's on the **subway**?

Melvin: "He's on the subway." I took the subway before! Why not? Dig where

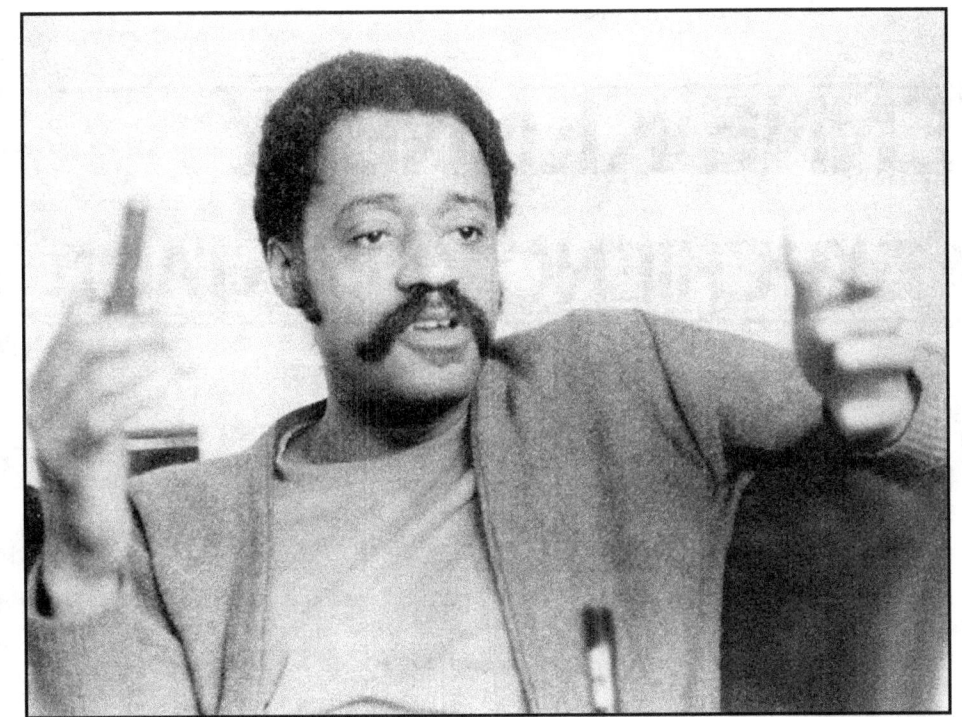

Photo by Bob Bryan

I'm coming from. When you take the subway, or when you wait for the bus . . .that's where that song that I wrote called "Just Don't Make No Sense". . . if I didn't wait for the bus, I'd forget about that. Maybe, I think that experience is too indelible in ones memory to forget. It creates a whole schizophrenia, a whole paranoia, trying to forget, but if you can pull all that together, then you're in business.

Bob: Do you deliberately go out after new experiences?

Melvin: No, man! I don't have to go after no new experiences. I step outside and a new experience grabs me. "Hey." Always some trouble. The other night I was at a girlfriends. She was asleep and I couldn't get in, and I'm trying to. I ain't got the key, and I'm trying to get to a telephone. One telephone don't work, another telephone, and the hawk is out there, kickin ass and takin' names (laugh). That's a new experience! So just by living, if you don't insulate yourself, you've got all the experience you need. So then I go into a bar, and I put a dime in, and the phone don't work, and I'm beginning to get the number and a bouncer comes over, "Hey, man, you stayin' or you goin'?" "Well, wait, man, I'm just. . ." "I think that you tryin' to avoid the cover charge and listen to the music." I said, "Naw, man, look, how much is the cover?" "Naw, I don't want the money, I just don't like to be. . ." Now he's gonna go through a whole thing. . . "Look, man, I'll pay the cover, just let me put the dime in here, in the phone, would ya please mistuh, please, huh?" You don't have to. . .just livin' there's enough goin' on out there, right? Step out on the corner and there's an old rag lady, who, "Yes, who gon shoot their neighbor?" You know what I mean?

Bob: But you know that you don't have to go through certain kinds of experiences because you're financially solvent; that you could ride around in a limousine, if you were into that. In a way, you must be **in there but out there**.

Melvin: Yeah but I enjoy it. Hey, man I enjoy talkin' to people, goin' here, goin' there. I'm pretty much of a hermit. I'm very seldom ever seen, 'cause I got a lot of work to do. The writing aspect, which is my power base, is a very long, drawn-out process. People often ask me, and very nicely so, "When you gonna do something else, brotha man?" Well, it's different if I am just acting, because you go from one thing to another, or directing is a little longer time, 'cause it takes a longer span for a movie and so forth. But your writing is an even longer span, and to even keep any kind of pace, I have to work seven days a week, man. I work seven days a week.

Bob: Do you live and work in this office?

Melvin: Naw. . .well more or less I do. I don't have a place, I haven't had a place for years. I'm a bachelor; well, I'm a divorce.

Cal: In the notes to the paperback version of **Sweetback**, you said that you did not want to be didactic. In other words, you wanted to be entertaining, understanding that you know that people have already been brainwashed So, expecting that. In your song, **There**, would you agree that that's an example

of what you were getting at? Rather than coming right out and saying that the brother beats up on his wife *because* of the nine to five job, you just express that.

Melvin: That is right, exactly, one hundred percent right. And if you can put it to a beat where people can nod their head and dig it and get the message. . .whereas, I could have said "I would like to explain to you so forth and so on" (affects snoring). I wanted to make a political film to explain some of the realities of Black America. Now, the vocal people who were down and raising hell, the elitists who decided the way the revolution was going to be run. . . When you start getting any kind of togetherness on another level, that they haven't decided, everybody gets pissed. You know what I mean, a guy says, well, hook shots won't work. A guy says, "Hey, man, I just made four points for us with two good hooks." Instead of him saying, "Yea for the team," he says, "Ahh shit. You're a revisionist!" You dig it?

Bob: Your ideas seem to have been ahead of your time. Do you think that most people are ahead of their time, but hold back for the sake of conformity?

Melvin: Well, I don't know if I am ahead of my time; I like to think of myself as timeless. If we would just stop and think about the hypes the man has laid on us. . . Remember the song, the last song in **Ain't Supposed to Die A Natural Death**, *Put A Curse On You*. Every time you get hip to the old one, the man lays a new hype on you. You see, my decision was that first I would try to make it possible for us to have technicians, and then I would not dictate to those technicians the political move that they would have to take. I'm just gonna try to get the food to the folks mouths. "Stay loose." We say this all the time, we use these words, and then

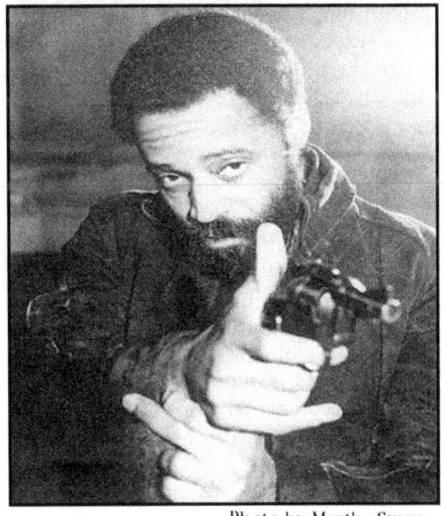

Photo by Martha Swope

Cont'd on page 55

ADRIENNE KENNEDY
THE DREAM EXPERIENCE ON STAGE

Strolling through a landscape of dreams, she finds that each road is many roads, that each dream is many dreams; that each mind that has blossomed in this country of illusion is actually many minds. Eyes stare at this sensitive, remarkable lady, who walks on, sometimes in fear; owl's eyes, that question her, that make her one with the African-based rituals which she creates. She stares back, into the owl's eyes, into the mist of multiple identities which she sees in us all.

"For a long time, I've been working to create a dreamlike experience in theatrical form," says Adrienne Kennedy, the playwright whose work *Funnyhouse of a Negro* remains a classic of the stage. "The mystical experiences, the experiences in the subconscious, are the real experiences in life. I write about the dream experience because I consider it to be the true state. I feel strongly that what goes on in our subconscious is what is really going on with us."

Adrienne Kennedy has achieved tremendous success in integrating her perceptions of the world with an acute sense of stagecraft. To see one of her plays, whether *A Beast Story* or *A Rat's Mass*, is to open yourself to an entirely different concept of theater, a concept which Adrienne sees as having a lot to do with one's ideas anout Man and how he interacts with his environment. Her belief is that our environment determines to a great extent our psychological make-up, which, in turn, results in each of us being possessed with many identities of equal validity.

"We all experience life on a number of levels, and I try to express this in my plays. I think there's a great ritual in all of my plays. As a matter of fact, going to Africa very much influenced my writing. I spent a lot of time watching the dancers; I feel that all of the African dancers are masterful at revealing people's feelings and the different levels of our existence."

A major theme in Adrienne's work is the transition of Southern Blacks into a Northern life style. Her parents, with

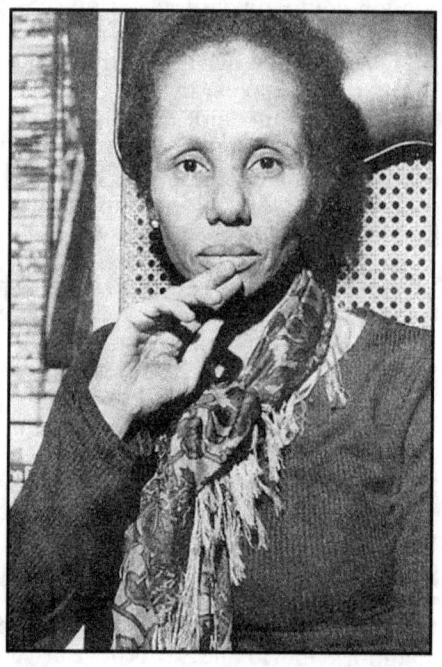

Photo by Leisant Giraux

whom she identifies greatly, were both from Georgia originally before moving to Cleveland, and her family experiences provide the roots for many of her theatrical explorations: "I'm very much my parents' child, still, and so a lot of what I write is about their lives." Adrienne feels strongly that "when

> "I write about the dream experience because I consider it to be the true state."

Article by
Cal Wilson

Black people moved to the North, a lot of their values were lost. Someone like my grandmother had values that were in many ways superior to today's standards."

Adrienne Kennedy had already been writing for some time, and had already penned *Funnyhouse of a Negro*, when she entered Edward Albee's playwriting class in the early Sixties. Her determination in reaching full fruition as a writer had carried her through a frustrating search for her own voice.

"I had been sort of discouraged because my plays were all short, and people said that my writing was fragmented. They kept telling me that it was important for me to write a full-length play. I had tried writing full-length plays, but I wasn't happy with any of them. Edward Albee helped me by encouraging me to continue to write in the vein in which I was writing."

When, with the assistance of Albee, she had *Funnyhouse* done at Actor's Studio, Adrienne found that her theatrical voice spoke clearly enough to develop a cult following around the play. Subsequently, after many workshop productions, *Funnyhouse of a Negro* was produced professionally Off-Broadway receiving the Village Voice Off-Broadway (Obie) Award.

Largely autobiographical in content, *Funnyhouse of a Negro* deals with a young Black woman's search for her identity. Through encounters with fantasy figures such as the Duchess of Hapsburg and Queen Victoria Regina, the central character of the play comes to understand the influences of European values upon her life and the contradictions inherent in a Black woman being forced to live out her life in an environment alien to those forces which gave her life.

"I've always tried to write about the racial situation as it affected me personally. My father, whom I worshipped, was a social worker. I've always been aware of all of the social issues, partly because of his influence. But when I set out to write about social issues, it wasn't real." Her plays emphasize psychology over sociology.

A notable exception is Adrienne's play, *An Evening With Dead Essex*. A departure from her other work, Essex deals with the life and death of Mark Essex, the young Black man who several years ago lost his life while sniping from atop a building in the South. Adrienne sees Essex as "a hero of a kind. Mark Essex was a very sensitive person who really felt many, many things. And rather than regarding him as perhaps some people do, who think that he lost his mind or *went off*, I feel that he made a conscious choice about his life. He gave a great deal of thought to what he was going to do, which I find admirable. You know that you're going to be killed if you go up on a tower and start shooting at people."

Produced at Yale University (where Adrienne lectured in playwriting as part of a fellowship), *An Evening With Dead Essex* was constructed in a documentary style, incorporating the use of slides. *Essex* was born partly out of Adrienne's fascination with journalism: "I went through a long period when I felt that the newspaper was the most exciting thing to pick up, and I still think that journalism presents greater drama than can be found in fiction. I always wanted to capture that quality of drama in a play."

"in *An Evening With Dead Essex*, I dealt with the political nature of our society. But I was also interested in Essex as a person; how he evolved from a quiet, reflective person with absolutely no inclinations toward violence into the sniper on the tower. I was interested in the violence in this society which caused him to take such action. I feel that he was a victim."

Essex was not her first attempt at documentary drama:

"The person I really wanted to write about was Malcolm X, and I tried and tried but I never could figure out how to do it. I wrote a lot of stories, I gathered lots of material, I had a lot of notebooks that I carried, but I never could come up with anything that satisfied me. Then I tried to do a play about George Jackson, and I found it very difficult because I

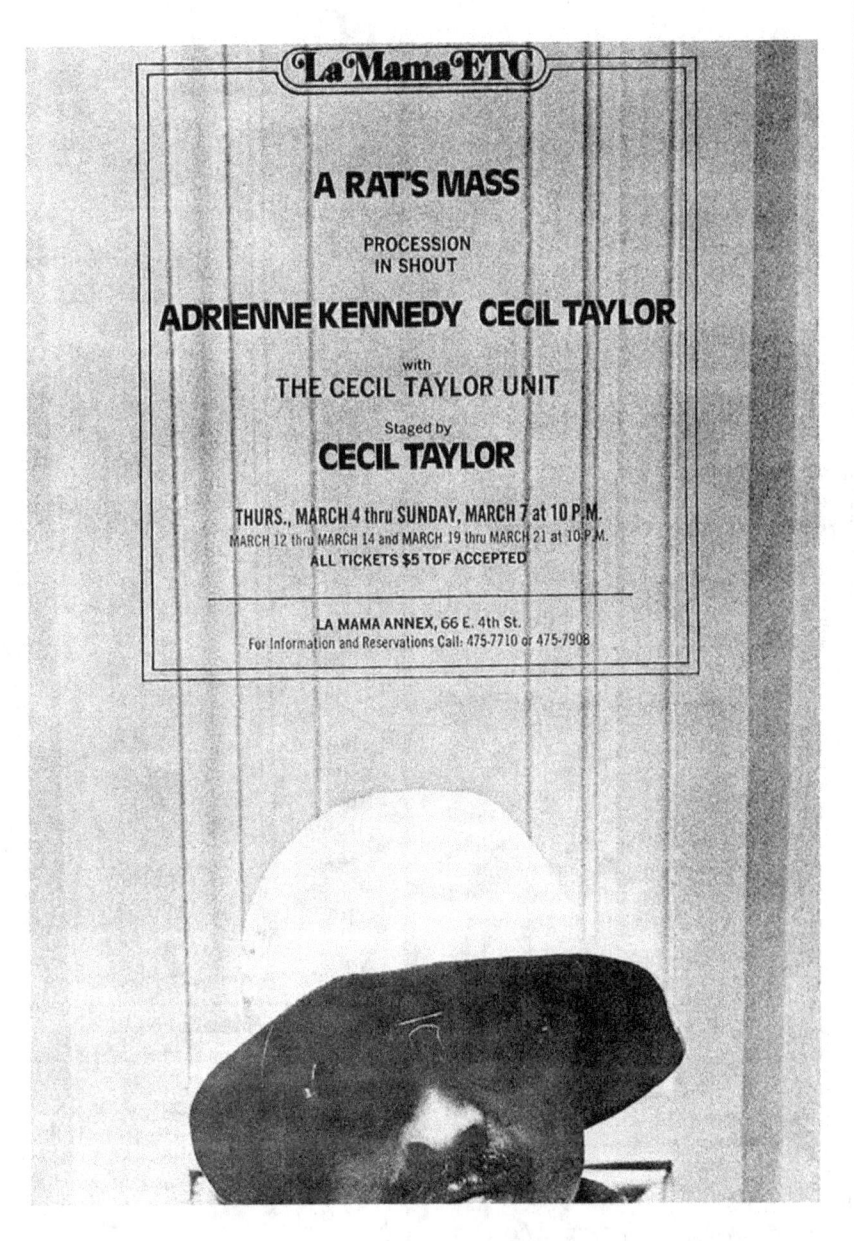

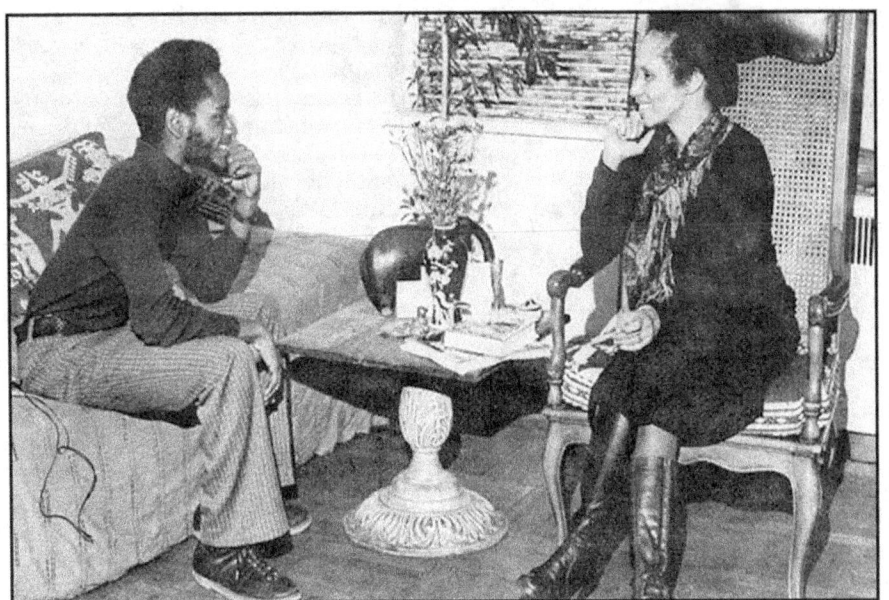

Cal Wilson and Adrienne Kennedy.

Photo by: Leisant Giraux

couldn't figure out how to write a play about somebody whose face was so familiar."

In the case of *An Evening With Dead Essex*, she solved that problem of writing about someone whose face was already known:

"I hit upon the idea of actors rehearsing a play about Essex, along with the use of slides from the newspapers. Thus the problem of having an actor impersonate him was eliminated."

Although Adrienne has not yet written a play about Malcolm X, she did write a play called *Sun* which is dedicated to his memory. A poetic stage piece, one of the symbols in *Sun* is a man whose spirit is eternal.

In some of her plays, such as *A Lesson in Dead Language* and *A Rat's Mass*, Adrienne Kennedy makes use of animal imagery. She feels that all of these animals are symbols, and the key to these images is rooted in the subconscious.

"I think I have a basic fear of certain kinds of animals; I certainly have a fear of rats. *A Rat's Mass* evolved from a dream that I had in a very crucial moment of my life. I was in Italy, on a train going to Rome, and at a time when I had been so happy, I had a nightmare of being chased by red, bloody rats. I keep notes on many of my dreams; the notes evolve into paragraphs, and two or three paragraphs might form the basis of a play. I think that, in *A Rat's Mass*, the rats definitely represent suppressed fear. On the other hand, in *A Lesson in Dead Language*, there's a little dog which symbolizes happiness.

"I've always been frightened by owls. There were some in my grandmother's garden, and I saw a lot of owls every day when I was living in Africa. *The Owl Answers* is partly rooted in that animal, that image."

Taking inspiration from Garcia Lorca (who wrote the classic play, *Blood Wedding*), Adrienne is deeply involved in developing the concept of presenting poetry in theatrical form. Her most recent success was the production at La Ma Ma E.T.C. Annex of a new version of *A Rat's Mass*, on which she collaborated with celebrated pianist Cecil Taylor. The experience could best be described as a pageant of dance, music, and ritual, touching upon such themes as the search for identity, Christianity, and the continuation of African culture in the Americas. Taylor's score, haunting in its beauty, perfectly complemented Kennedy's rich, enthralling book.

"I think writing is a God-given talent. I happen to have been given that particular role, to write. I feel fortunate that I was given something specific to do." ✿

POETRY

Lonely brother,
Walking in the Shadows
of Isolation and Confusion.
An Obscure Darkness
that Blinds Him from the Specter
of That Brighter Day.
Whose Pace
is a Drag
of Slow Death
of No Interest
of No Hope
Face,
Whose Once Youthful Luster
has Now been Replaced
by Black Hairs of Time and Wrinkles.
NO, NO WORSE
Grooves of Ploughed Ditches
Collecting Decaying Forms
of Lifeless Bodies
Thrown into a Mass-Gravesite of Stench
And EYES. . .EYES
That Stare
Hypnotically
At the Unbroken Path of Asphalt.
EYES
That Occassionally Look-Up
To Find Themselves
IN the Same Sea of Horrid Human
    Insanity
THE LOOK THAT HE FEARS
Turns His Head
Back Down
To The COLD,
UNFEELING
Yet FRIENDLY
Street of Stone
That Envelopes His Being
In a rapport of NOTHINGNESS.
Isolating
His Feeling of Non-Existence
To Isolate Himself
Within The Shadows of a World
That Rejected
And NOW
TERRORIZES
HIM.

Robert Bryan
Paris '72

black love

you don't need
a great talk
to see
how important
you are for me
it's not worth while
I say I love
your eyes
your mouth
your body
what you do
what you say
it's not worth while

I tell you
our story with thrill
in my voice
Oh! no
gently
I put my hands on your face
And whisper
Oh! How I love you!

Josiane Broche

Josiane Broche is a poet born in Martinque: she is now living in Paris.

something out of you

you keep asking me if i want
something out of you
but if i didn't
why should i be here?
here
with you
and all your hints of suspicion
and all your nuances of compassion
which mix themselves
and me
up
in amazement
but show me nothing
of your love
something out of you
is what i want
or maybe
all i want is you
or
maybe
these two things are the same
but i have to go to work now
so i'll leave you for the train
so i'll leave you
looking
as i look for
something out of you

Calvin Wilson
New York City 1975

36

The Power of Art

Dr. Ademola Talks About His Work

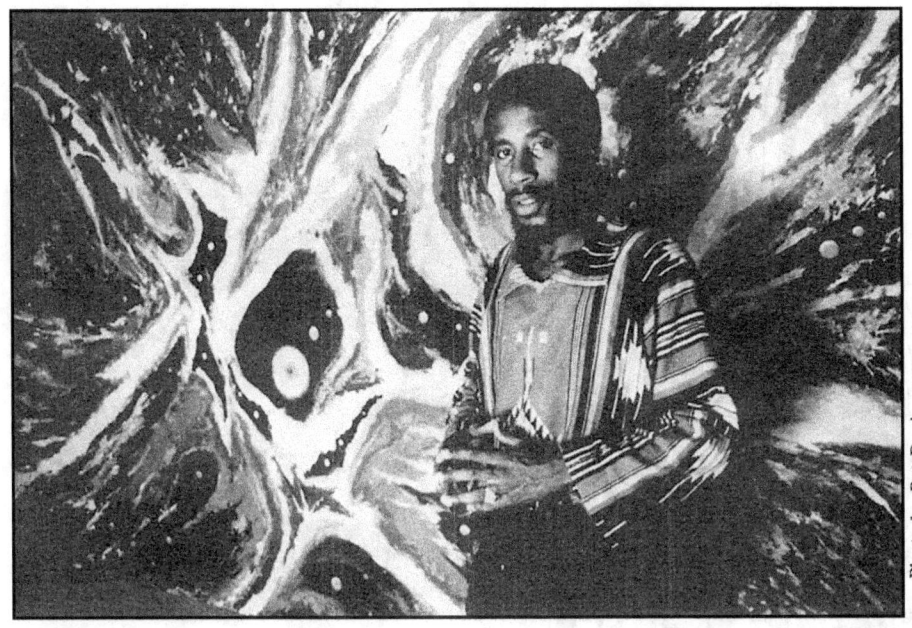

Photo by Pat Davis

I am basically trying to express, or, I should say, raise the consciousness of, the observer. By this I mean, I want to be able to create visual equations that make a person think. Very often, when people relate to art, especially Black people at this particular time, they're looking for things that are very representational, or pictorial, and this is fine. However, in many instances, it does not leave room for the imagination, and I think that art should invoke imagination and leave room for the imagination to really flow. With a direction, however.

That's very important, and I stress direction because, if that isn't the case, then you have just art for art's sake. I am specifically working on a series of works based on the Orionic principle. That principle is based on the premise that we have evolved from another space, or, for lack of a better word, another universe, and that in our evolving from this other space we lost some of the overt mind powers that we once possessed. By this I mean that we had a very highly developed intellectual atomic capacity, being able to control the molecules of our existence. We were in a higher state, more of an ether existence, which is a much higher state than we are now in physically. So things such as astral traveling, disintegration of the

body, self-healing—all of these areas were commonplace within our culture at one point. Of course, I'm going back possibly trillions of years, which really was just a second ago in terms of what time is really about. And, not meaning to sound way-out, but I believe that the visual sciences can, in fact, invoke some of those lost powers, because they really are not lost in the total sense of the word; they have been subdued.

There's a universal law I'm sure everyone has heard of, that there's nothing new under the sun. Well, I think that's very real. Everything, even plus and minus, if you add something, it means something you're taking away from something else. So nothing really changes in terms of mass, space or volume that it occupies, and it's the same way with consciousness. What has happened is, in becoming more physical, some of the intuitive powers, some of the mental powers, that we possessed were subdued. Myself and other artists who are in my vein of thinking are hoping to invoke and awaken some of those dormant chambers of the mind. This particular vein of thinking, I guess, has always been lying dormant in my head.

Many years ago, I was dealing with

music, with an organization called Pomusicart, and one of the objects of the organization was to unite the art forms into a spontaneous movement, thereby bringing a whole new aura to artistic expression, and, ultimately, to Black people's consciousness. So it's nothing new in that sense. However, my visual work has taken a sudden turn towards more astral space-like qualities since, I would say, 1970. That year represented a kind of a turning point in my art. I think that my art is speaking for today.

Now, most people who have studied my evolution since the early '60's have seen that my work has gone through a number of changes. In the '60's specifically, my work was extremely graphic; it was extremely "African-oriented." Very, very sharp linear works. A lot of my works were based on my study of African art, so thereby many of the mass forms were integrated into the work. There was also a period when I began to work with shells and rope and traditional things that you had found in African sculpture, but in a new way. And of course, this was the art of the '60's. At that point it was very, very important to the masses of Black people, who I am really concerned with, to see this. It was kind of a re inforcement of their Blackness or even an awakening to their Blackness through the art form.

I also had another objective, and that was to instill the African idiom firmly into the Black art movement of the '60's. I was very successful in being able to do that. However, I think that you have to move past just discovering your Blackness or revelling in your Blackness, and you have to move to another level which is always, of course, geared towards nationhood. And in 1970, I didn't intellectually say, well, I'm going to change my work; it just happened that way, because I've always been, I feel, attuned to universal changes, and the '70's signaled a new turn in thinking. We had reached a point where we had discovered our Blackness, and were now proud of our Blackness. It's time to begin to synthesize and expand our thoughts, and this is what my art is attempting to do.

I've been getting excellent response from people who I would have normally thought wouldn't dig what I'm doing, but it seems that I am on the right track, because I am getting reactions from people all across the board, people who've never seen art before and never really paid attention to it, or found a lot of room for their expression within my work, and I think that's very, very important. If you notice, within a lot of the pieces there is a symbol that I've

Cont'd on page 53

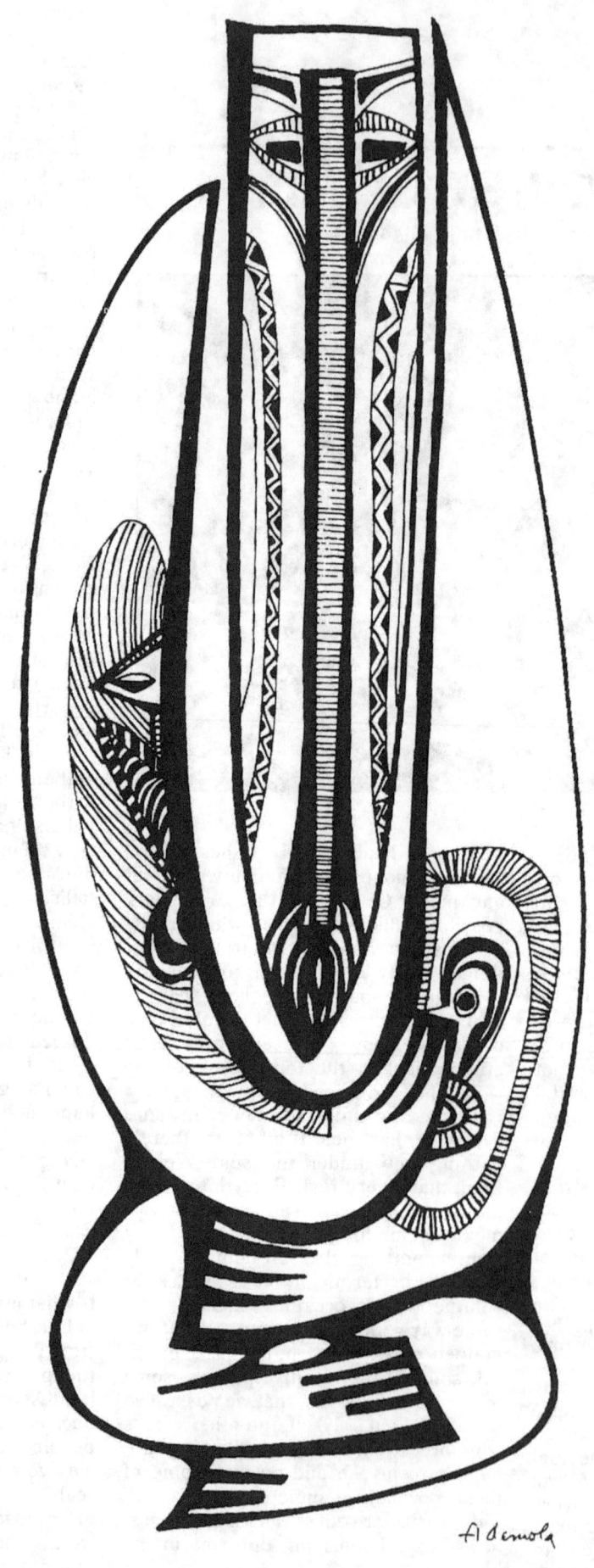

Ancestor Energy
(woodcut - 1968)

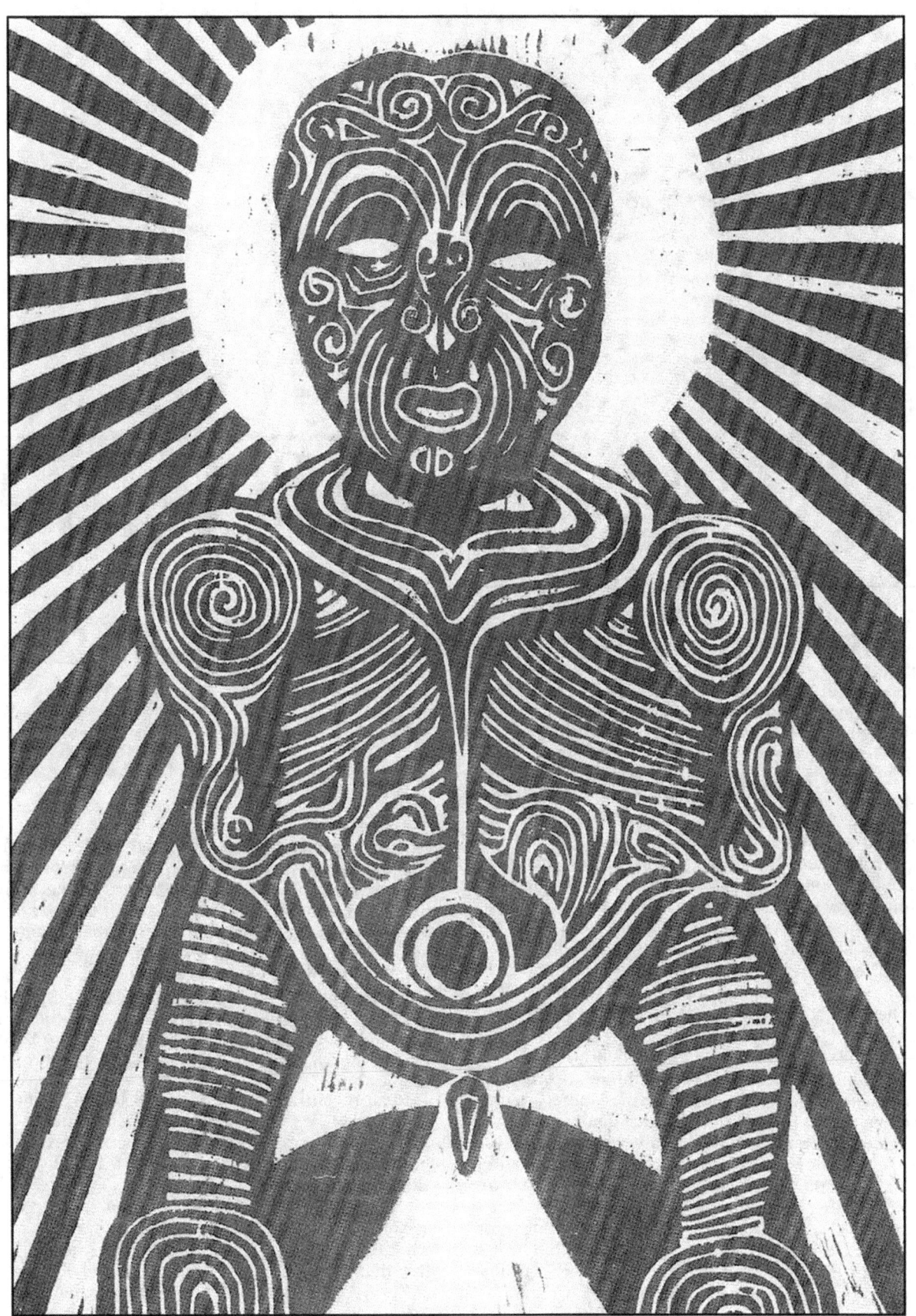

Dr. Ademola's work can be see at the Benin Gallery at 2366 Seventh Avenue, New York City.

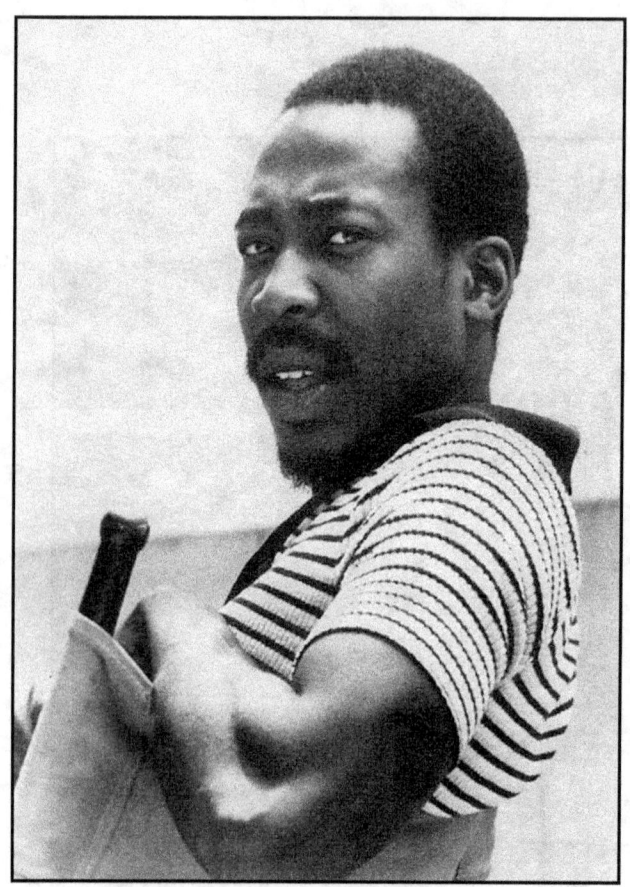

BRENT JENNINGS

"My goal is to be as totally involved in the realities of the performing arts business as possible."

The speaker is Brent Jennings, one of the busiest actors in New York City. And the realities of which he speaks are the rapidly expanding opportunities for Black actors to get involved in the produciton end of the theatrical world. Brent has a long list of acting roles to his credit, as well as directorial experience. He spent two seasons with the Theater Company of Boston. During this time he appeared as Nicknack in Edgar White's *The Burghers of Calais* and as Parham in *The Basic Training of Pavlo Hummel*. Brent worked as an actor and director with the New African Company, and for the past two summers has lent his acting abilities to the Eugene O'Neil National Playwrights Conference.

Just a few years ago, Brent was making a very good living as an advertising executive, but the time came when he had to decide on what he really wanted to do with his life. His desire to act won out: "I felt isolated and unfulfilled in the work I was doing. Finally, I decided to make the necessary commitment to acting, which meant I had to forget about fine clothes, sports cars and going to the Bahamas for vacations."

These days, Brent Jennings hardly has time for vacations. Not only is he constantly busy as an actor, having appeared or starred in such plays as *Ode to Charlie Parker* by Edgar White and *The Past Is the Past* by Richard Wesley, but he is also an active member of Voices, Inc., a musical theater company. Through his involvement with the company, he says, he is learning "how to put a company together and keep it together. To me, my experience in working with the artists involved in Voices Inc. invaluable."

lifelines

Brent received most of his theatrical training in Boston(he holds a B.S. degree in speech from Emerson College) and the move to New York City was a big step in hisdevelopment as an actor. He admits that he was a bit apprehensive about making the move, but "a cat who taught me in Boston once told me that if you stick with it say five, six years, something will work out." He feels that his time in New York City has helped him to grow: New York would prepare you for the grimmer side of life." The changes he has gone through in order to cope with his new environment have fed directly into his art.

Most recently, Brent apperared in *Bargainin' Thing* at the New Federal Theater. As he continues to work and refine his craft, Brent Jennings remains mindful of his role in insuring the future of a healthy, exciting Black Theater.

"I feel that Black Theater is very much alive. There are many aspects of our existence in this country which we haven't dealt with in a dramatic way." He feels that theater can help us to explore ourselves.

Brent Jennings has confidence. As he moves into the future, he will continue to move *us*—with each performance. —C.W. ✡

SONIA MANZANO

Last summer, I attended a performance of a play called, *The Commitment*, which was being presented at the New Federal Theater on East Third Street. The play sought to deal realistically with Puerto Rican life in New York City, and I could tell from the reaction of the largely Puerto Rican audience that most of the spectators, young and old, were digging where the play was coming from. The energy in the audience was high, and everyone was intensely involved with the action on stage.

All was quiet in the theater. On stage, a young woman was holding out her hand to two actors who were, in this space and time, her mother and brother. On the ring finger of her hand, a ring shone, brightly, but not as brightly as the smile of the young woman, an actress named Sonia Manzano. And when, on a crest of ecstasy, Sonia announced her engagement and forthcoming marriage, the audience rode the feeling *con mucho gusto* —all could appreciate the truth of the episode.

The smile on Sonia's face as she continued her performance was due to much more than simply the successful rendering of a scene. The smile was one of fulfillment: as an artist, as a woman, as everything she considers herself to be.

Born in the South Bronx, Sonia Manzano discovered her talent for acting early, at the New York High School of the Performing Arts. It was there that she met Vinette Carroll, whom she credits with further spurring her on to see what acting is all about.

Out of all of the directions in the arts which were available to her, Sonia chose acting because it appealed to her the most: "I remember saying to myself, 'If this little bit feels this good, a lot more is going to feel a lot better.'" Determination and hard work paid off: Sonia was an original cast member of *Godspell* and has been a regular on *Sesame Street* since its debut five years ago.

Looking back on her involvement in *The Commitment*, Sonia feels that it was an important step in her career. Her success in *Godspell* had opened the doors to Broadway, but Sonia found herself less than satisfied with the roles being offered to her. Her role in *The Commitment* provided her with the kind of depth that she prefers to deal with in developing a character.

"Maybe two years ago, if someone had asked me if I wanted to do a showcase, I would have said, 'Not really,' but now I feel that Nuyoricans have to start making theater a New York phenomenon for Puerto Ricans, like *salsa*."

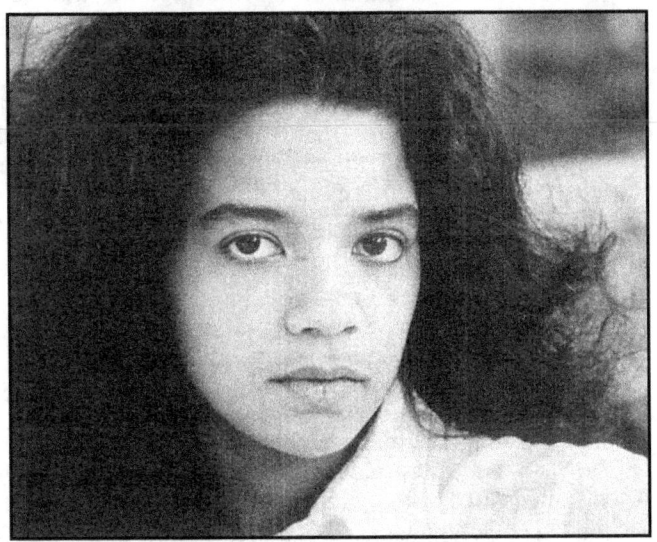

Photo by Jimmy Baylor

It was during her involvement in *The Commitment* that Sonia decided to channel her energies into the development of a New York-based Puerto Rican theater. The move was partly one of personal necessity—she got tired of the stereotypes of Puerto Rican woman that she was being fed while "making the rounds" on Broadway. "I always felt like I was being used as commodity. Finally, I realized that I've got to express myself, and I can't do that being a symbol."

In sharp contrast, she finds that her role as Maria on *Sesame Street* allows her the freedom to be natural. She sees the series as a positive educational tool.

"I can remember, as a little girl, lying in bed at night and trying to imagine shapes and figures out of the cracks in the ceiling. *Sesame Street* gives kids more than a cracked ceiling to deal with."

Sesame Street has provided Sonia with the "one foot in the established world" from which she plans to aid other artists in getting their work into the commercial arena. She is particularly concerned with seeing honest depictions of Puerto Rican life on television, and feels that many of the writers she has been meeting at workshops in New York City should have a stronger voice over the airwaves. But she advises these writers to remember what television is really about when writing for the medium: "They want a brown or a black 'Mary Tyler Moore Show.' The people in the television industry don't want to bring in people that they don't understand, because as soon as they don't understand them, they don't want to deal with them."

Concerning her approach to acting, Sonia feels that actors are similar to musicians, in that it is the responsibility of both to find room for improvisation.

"When dealing with the script, I treat the words as a series of notes. It's up to me to interpret those notes as well as I can. When I'm really playing well, it's a freeing experience—like jazz."

Acting makes Sonia "feel great. I really feel as if I have no choice but to act." From her acting teacher, Robert Patterson, she learned that discipline is important, but "you can't take yourself too seriously. If you think acting is sacred, you won't get off on it."

To those who would criticize Puerto Rican theater for perhaps giving too much exposure to some of the negatives elements in the culture, Sonia points out that "when in one year there are only about three plays produced, you can't cover the whole experience in these three plays, or expect the writers to." She would like to see more Puerto Rican businessmen become involved in theatrical producing.

Sonia will be appearing soon in *The Sun Always Shines For The Cool*, a new play by Miguel Pinero, who wrote *Short Eyes*. This new Pinero work, like the award-winning *Short Eyes*, will be directed by Marvin Felix Camillo. Sonia considers Camillo "an actor's director. He really wants you to act." If the response to the recent workshop production of *The Sun Always Shines For The Cool* is any indication, Pinero and Camillo have another hit on their hands. The success of the play is due in no small part to Sonia's magnificent performance in the leading female role.

Sonia Manzaho's energy is high. Her talent is more than overwhelming, and her confidence and drive in communicating through her art should keep her on the scene for a long time to come.

"Tell yourself whatever you need to tell yourself," she says, commenting on her will to succeed. "That's between you and yourself." —C.W✿

Anna Josephine had been a spoiled child; she loved the memory of her mischievous youth. She had matured as a strong, positive woman, and this was due to the influence of her older sister Marilyn. Marilyn had taken care of Anna from age nine to seventeen. Marilyn did a lot of strict, moral living as an example for her baby sister. Their mother had led the way, howver. Still, Kay had wanted Marilyn to be as "fine" a young lady as she had been. A month after her seventeenth birthday, Anna married William Choteau O'Brian. "Bill", as he preferred to be called, was a Scot-Irishman of twenty-six years. Anna had changed her hair color from sandy brown to red when she was fifteen. It had complemented her copper-brown skin color. She was indeed the daring woman of the family, while her sister had always taken life in order, and in its stride. Anna Josephine was large-boned; she was two inches taller than Marilyn. She had gone from 115 pounds, as a young woman, to 138, now in her 33rd year. Anna and Bill had decided that they would not have children, but if they had, they would have been as unorthodox and Bohemian as their mother and fatehr had been. After her marriage to Bill, Anna allowed her hair to resume its natural color. At the present time, however, she preferred to wear jet-black wigs. Anna and Bill separated after seven years as husband and wife. Marilyn asked her to come back home with her and her mother.

So the three women, the mother and her two daughters, once again dwelled together in their four-and-a-half rooms on Christopher Street. Kay occupied the living room, Marilyn gave her room to Anna, and Marilyn occupied her mother's master bedroom.

Anna had brought her own bedroom furniture to put into the room, in which she had seldom slept as a child. Marilyn had found it difficult to part with her mother's first bedroom set. It had seen much usage in its days of usefulness, and it showed the signs of scrawling that children are likely to imitate. The furniture had been of the Colonial period. Its red-orange hue was enriched by the bright silk sea-blue bedspread set and curtains, which long ago helped to decorate the room. The walls were a pale yellow, then. The entire apartment was now a pale green. Marilyn often walked from her bedroom to the eggshell-colored kitchen, observing the flash of primary and secondary colors as she did. Her room was decorated in red. Her mother's bedroom set was dated, as it was designed out of a style of the early 50's. It had been the second bedroom set purchased by Kay.

Kay updated the living room with new, expensive furniture every ten years. Its decor was presently of reds, greens, oranges, and yellows. The dining room, also refurnished every ten years, followed the color scheme; in fact, repeated it. Marilyn had promised Kay that during the next decade, or sooner, she would purchase furniture for the entire apartment. Kay had given all verbal indications that she would wait for it. Marilyn had always had big plans for her mother and sister. She believed that they would see better days and she constantly expressed her belief. Marilyn was drowned out by both of them whenever she spoke this way. (It was Marilyn, however, who had promised, too, to buy a hone in West Virginia, or North Carolina, Marilyn's and Anna's place of birth, upon Kay's retiring from hospital work.) Marilyn didn't like being shut up in this manner, but she hoped that someday she could live up to her big talk.

While at Brooklyn State, the South Beach Psychiatric Center had taken over her case. In fact, they had tried to aid her during the latter stages of her approaching "breakdown" by coming to her mother's house, counseling her and giving her medication. This didn't help. When she was taken to the the hospital, they placed her under semi-private therapy. After she was released, she was assigned a therapeutic nurse. Mrs. Tannihill and Doctor Oxley had been her nurse and psychiatrist before she was committed. Marion Lee had now been assigned.

Before leaving, or being discharged from, Brooklyn State Hospital, she had signed a paper which had admitted her to a technical training program. She was to be put "in-training" for office skills. After she came home, she never missed a session with Miss Lee. Marion gave her a vocabulary, math, and spelling test within weeks of her arrival home. Still, she waited for about nine months before she was sent to the C.F. Young Secretarial School. C.F. Young was nearly a mile from the Green Horn Housing Projects, in which she had then lived for 18 years.

Marilyn Betsey Cummings never missed a day at secretrial school. She attended C.F. Young, which was a school for women, for about a year. Still, just as Marion never invited her to socialize outside of their sessions, (as Marion was only five years old than she) none of the girls at school ever invited her to their parties, or to their homes. Just as with Marion, however, Marilyn never asked. This inability to gain friends would continue.

Marilyn terminated the sessions with her nurse after physical complications resulted; she believed the medication to be the cause. She had begun bleeding from the vagina. Marion refused to change the medication, and Marilyn sought help at a neighboring clinic. At about that time, November, 1971, she also left C.F. Young. They had never allowed her to join in on the speed sessions in shorthand, they had tried to push her around, and she had found the school very pressure-oriented. She vowed never to enroll at a non-credited school again.

Because of the refresher course in bookeeping which she had had at C.F. Young, she was able to get a job at Abraham & Straus' department store. She was a saleswoman in the Lingerie Department. Marilyn was supposed to have the job through the Christmas Season. Although she could hardly walk after a day on her feet, she soaked them in hot, epsom salt water nightly and returned to work ready the next day. Still, she loved working with and around people. She was never late—again, she attended work daily, but this was for the amount of time that she was allowed to work. On her sixth day at A&S, a supervisor from another part of the store came down to her counter with a $50 bill, asked her to go into stock (where the item that she wanted couldn't be found), then began an argument with her. Since Marilyn knew that she wasn't required to take a bill that large, and she wasn't supposed to go into stock, she told the woman, who was Irish, to go to Hell. That supervisor told the management that Marilyn had gone into a fit, and called her out of her name, as Marilyn strowed clothing everywhere. Well! Marilyn was fired, not being given adequate reasons why; but she was glad that she'd told that bitch where she belonged. Yes, she had tried to agree with the "system", but she would try harder.

During the month of December, she went over to Hunter College to apply for admission. She entered for the Spring semester, 1972. However, she couldn't afford more than one subject, which was Typing I. She had figured that she would gain enough speed to be able to get a job for the summer. Her plans didn't materialize, but she did get a "B" for the course.

On March 1, while changing from the IRT local at 59 Street to the Lexington Avenue Express, she met Bill Harriston. He was a tall, well-built man of 38 years. Marilyn had become 31 the day before. Bill's face was like sunshine. As they piled into the crowded express train, he said something her. She loved his attention. Bill had a moderate-sounding voice, and rather excellent diction. As they stood pressed next to one another, he tried to speak above the noise of the train. Marilyn found this gesture odd, and comedic, but she complied. It was the happiest train ride she had ever taken on the Lexington Avenue. As she gazed into his brown eyes, through his gold-framed spectacles, he said, "You like the sun, don't you?" She said, yes, and tried to add conversation to his non-sensible questions, but in fact she adored the sun; it was the only warmth she had known at many times in her life. Still, she didn't ask this reddish-brown stranger if he'd gotten a tan, though her mind rambled about doing so. At Fulton Street, he, too, changed for the "A" train. Oh! He was everything that she had ever wanted in a man. Handsom, with a stocky, beautiful body, a face like sunshine, and voice like music, and he was EDUCATED!!! She knew that he was the man for whom she had waited all of her life. She wanted him, terribly. The pain had become a throb, a pin-point in her "pubic victory" box. The ache was excruciating. She thought her whole body was in pain. Joyous, wonderful PAIN! She wanted to touch him, but she didn't want to give herself away.

When they arrived at High Street, he asked her at what station she got off. She told him, "Boro Hall." He got off, too. He asked her to come have dinner with him. She wanted to, but she refused. She asked him his name again, but the train was coming. Above the rumble, and the bang of screaming wheels, he yelled, "BILL HARRISTON!" She gave him her telephone number, and got on the "F" train. Marilyn had been anxious, but careful not to invite this darling gentleman to her mother's home before she had told her about him.

After arriving home, she tried to talk about Bill, all night. Her mother and sister didn't want to hear the blab, and furthermore, they didn't trust him. They warned her that he was probably some maniac, etc. It hurt Marilyn to hear him ridiculed in such a way, but she instantly became afraid of him. She wondered how Fate could be so cruel. She was lonely, and needed his kindness and love, if he wanted to give it. She held back the tears of her trying, needing, hungry soul.

The next morning, at about eleven, he called, but Marilyn was asleep. Her mother told her about his call explaining that she hadn't wanted to disturb her, and for that reason had not called her to the phone. Well! Marilyn went into a rage, demanding that her mother call her whenever someone wanted her on the telephone. But Marilyn knew that actually, no one had called her in years. She had especially not received any calls from men.

Somehow Marilyn and Bill got together again, and he again tried to invite her out to dinner. Again, she didn't accept. He told her that he would wait for her at Broadway-Nassau after school, the next session. He did.

As she came from the IRT down the last flight of stairs, she saw him parked against the stairwell. He was looking and, of course, she was looking. She felt ashamed of the shabby, worn-out clothing that she had to wear, as he was in an impressive, light-brown, English-tailored suit. It fit his chest and sinewy thighs as he was a weight-lifter. Everything bulged. Oh, oh, OH! Did she want him. When his gentle voice met her ears, she was READY! She died to tell him yes, yes, ...YES!

When she got to her stop, he got off with her. She felt sure of herself, and she was so proud to be seen with him. As the Eighth Avenue awaited the arrival of the entering Sixth Avenue train, he whispered to her, "Bye Luv!" When she glanced back, he was gone. She ran onto the end of the train. The sound of her heavy, plastic-soled shoes clip-clopped throughout the car. She had, actually, hoped that he would follow her, even though she had not asked him to. It "blew her mind," that she hadn't seen where he had disappeared. The ride home was soul-bending, as she could now understand what he had said to her.

Two weeks had passed; Bill had not called. When a month had dragged by, she began to pray that she would see him again. She had to have his beautiful love. Of course it would be beautiful, with him; he was heavenly, but she had forgotten what he looked like. Every man looked like Bill.

One afternoon when she didn't have class she had decided to wait for him in the subway station, in the very spot where he had waited for her that evening. She had said, to at least three men of varying shapes and sizes, "Bill?" They shook their heads, no. The crowded "rush-hour" trains had passed for two or three hours before she gave up. She had decided to paint a message near the stairway for the "A" train. No! She would write several messages, where he would likely spot them. "BILL, PLEASE CALL MARILYN. SHE LOVES YOU! CALL HOME!" No! She would write a part of the message on each stair level. She had decided that, in order to do this, she would get out during the early A.M., perhaps about three. But she knew that the police would arrest her if they caught her posting bills in the subway station. She didn't know what to do, but she continued to pray for his return, now more passionately than ever. She promised God that she would become a devout believer, if only she could have Bill's love. She knew that she had been a fool to listen to her mother, or her sister, or her Uncle Clyburn, or Celia, her best friend. None of them had liked the way in which she had met him; they had all warned her of horrible consequences. What could ever happen to her, to be more horrible, that this burning, crazed desire which she held for him? Nohting, nothing in this whole, wide world. Bill had told her that they didn't understand her at home, and she now agreed with him. Still, she could not have talked to him about what they had said, and she could not have talked to them about what he had said.

She had closed her eyes only slightly to his sexy, perverted talk on the phone, his asking her for money, or his attempt to persuade her to fly with him to his aunts in Cleveland, Ohio. She knew that he wasn't perfect, but she believed that he would never let any harm come to her innocence. She wondered where he was, and whether he was warm at night.

As she stood in the Broadway-Nassau station waiting for the train one afternoon, she happened to be looking in the direction of the stairs, and whom should she see, but BILL! She waited until he approached her. They exchanged small talk. She then invited him to her mother's home, after finding out that he wasn't in a

Cont'd on page 50

43

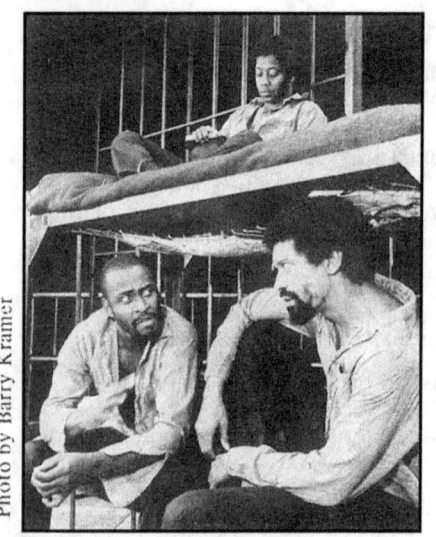

Photo by Barry Kramer

L to R: Clevon Little, Northern Calloway, Dick A. Williams.

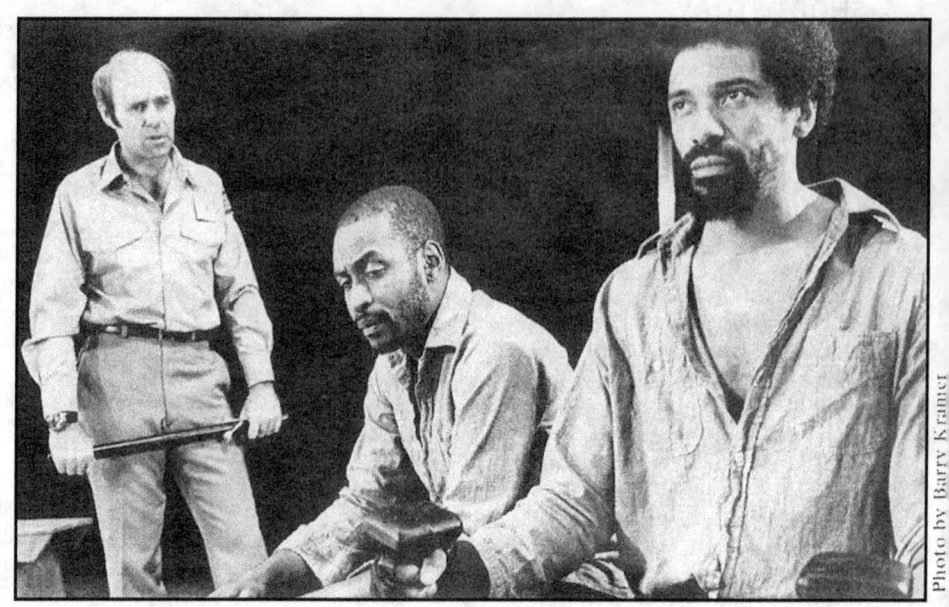

Photo by Barry Kramer

L to R: Peter Masterson, Clevon Little, Dick A. Williams.

Point of View: CLEAVON LITTLE   DICK A. WILLIAMS

Recently, at the Ambassador Theater, Cleavon Little and Dick Anthony Williams starred in Ronald Ribman's The Poison Tree.

An unusual play, The Poison Tree dealt with the deterioration of both prisoners and guards within the prison system.

Cleavon Little won the Tony Award for best actor for his performance in the hit musical Purlie. A versatile actor, Little has captured the television, movie

CLEAVON LITTLE

Bob Bryan: Do you think that the ideas being put out in *The Poison Tree* might turn off certain audiences?

Cleavon Little: Sure, there's some people who wouldn't want to deal with it because the truth of it may hit them personally, but that's really not the issue. I think that the closing of the play has something to do with critics who are not really aware of anything that's important contemporary-wise. This play is much bigger than just Blacks and Blacks in prison. And so, for that matter, I think that that's a whole different set of circumstances. I think the play can draw an enormous audience, but again our problem with this play, which is often a problem, with a lot of plays . . .this is the first play I've ever done in the past ten years of my whole career as an

Cont'd on page 47

and theater audiences. He has made guest appearances on The Waltons, The Rookies, and Police Story, and starred in his own series, Temperatures Rising. On the screen, Little starred in the phenomenally successful comedy Blazing Saddles. His stage career has ranged from the Off-Broadway play Scuba Duba to the recent Broadway hit All Over Town, directed by Dustin Hoffman.

Dick Anthony Williams is one of the fastest-rising young actors on the contemporary scene. Williams has twice been nominated for the Tony Award for his excellent portrayals in the Broadway plays Black Picture Show and What The Wine-Sellers Buy. For his performance in Wine-Sellers he received the Drama Desk, Tor and Audelco awards. He is the star of Woodie King, Jr.'s soon-to-be-released film The Long Night. Williams has also appeared in such films as Dog Day Afternoon, The Anderson tapes, Five on the Black Hand Side, The Mack, Up Tight, and Slaughter's Big Rip-Off (with Jim Brown). In addition, he is the author of the following plays: A Bit O' Black, which had successful runs in Chicago and Los Angeles; One, which was produced at the New Federal Theater (a theater which Williams co-founded); and the musical, Black and Beautiful. He co-wrote, directed and starred in the Off-

Broadway hit Big Time Buck White. At the New Federal Theater, he co-produced Martie Charles' Jamimma (in which he played the lead role) and Black Girl, which Ossie Davis later directed as a film. The Pig Pen, a play by Ed Bullins, was staged by Williams at the American Place Theater.

The following interviews took place between performances backstage in their dressing rooms at the Ambassador Theater during the production of The Poison Tree.

DICK ANTHONY WILLIAMS

Cal Wilson: You once said that you like to do plays that provoke people to think. In terms of this experience in the **Poison Tree**, what kind of ideas do you think are being put out for people to think about?

Dick Anthony Williams: You get an overview of the prison system; you don't just get a play about the black prisoners . . .that's an ordinary play. You get the prisoners and the guards, and you get to peep a small world that in a way is like the bigger world outside the prison. You come to understand that the guards and the prisoners are all enclosed within the walls, and that they both corrode. The people that they pick for guards are people who couldn't gig other places. You have to deal with a mentality that would become a guard and hold people under

44

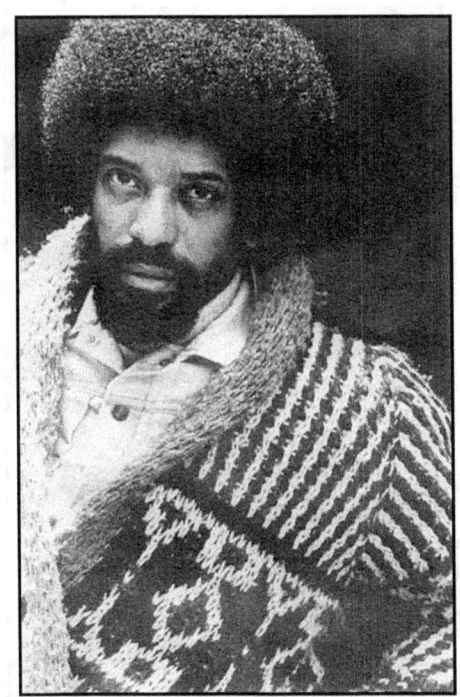

bondage for nice pay. And so the guards have sort of a camaraderie back and forth with the prisoners, but they're all incaged. It's like a microcosm of a macrocosm, because there's a spillover outside the prison into the system that we live in, which is another kind of prison where money talks; where graft is prevalent, and appointments are made, and not because of a person's talent. Where doctors become doctors simply because it's a profession where they can make a certain amount of money and get a certain amount of respect. It's not really about human beings.

Cal: There seemed to be a very clear-cut debate between the character you played and the character Cleavon Little played, in terms of just how to deal with the prison society, as well as the outside society. Do you think that either one of them won the argument, or do you think that the answer is somewhere in-between?

Dick: The answer may be somewhere in-between. Willie Stepp's character (Cleavon Little) is a guy that talks and looks toward the future; that believes in laying foundations, to do what you have to do. Bobby Foster (Dick Williams) is more immediate, more now. Both of them get ripped off in the end, both of them run into an impasse that you can't get beyond. Willie Stepp's whole thing is that, in a whole lifetime, he would not have done anything. In terms of Bobby Fosters' lifetime, he'll get killed. He'll kill a Hurspool (Moses Gunn); he'll kill a tom, and they'll kill him, and he wouldn't have been effective, except as a vestige of some kind of memory of a deed that he did that may or may not be

remembered. Probably the reason why he did the deed if its recorded in later history might become distorted, y'know what I mean. Y'know, like history is like his-story, whatever they decide to pick out as important. They say what happened during this period between 1800 and 1850 and they give you one incident that is usually about people warring with each other, and that is supposed to represent 50 years.

Bob Bryan: Do you feel that the character that you're playing substantially differs from some of the other characters that you've played before and how so?

Dick: Yeah. . .he's different! I guess he's different than all the rest, in a way. I think that even when you do one pimp, one pimp is different than another pimp. They're out there in the same area, but they are different people. This one is different in that he's quick to get down, and he thinks in terms of what he can do, and what he can do is fight. There are similarities between Bobby Foster in **Poison Tree** and a pimp like Rico in **What The Wine-Sellers Buy** (Author: Ron Milner). They are both men who will not be broken by a standardized society. They veer off in different ways; Bobby Foster will probably get killed, Rico will probably get killed. They are both anti-system men, in a sense. A pimp, he finds himself in a situation, he watches all these people who are apologizing for their existence and who are quiet. That's where he gets loud. (laugh) It's a whole 'nother philosophy that goes in. I don't know if any of this makes any sense.

Cal: It sounds as if there are some of the same elements in these characters as

there are in Alexander, in **Black Picture Show**.

Dick: Alexander is another character who refuses to be broken down and departmentalized and put in a category and left alone. I guess there are similarities in these men, 'cause Alexander is the kind of man who is a filmmaker, and an artist; who the system has turned very crazy, and, in a way, very sane. When you are dealing with an insane person, you don't deal with him as a person who is out of his head. You figure he's a person who is out of other people's frame of reference; they just can't deal with where he's coming from. The man is coming from someplace that I think is very dynamic. All of them are Black men. . .all of them are faced with all the pressures that a white society imposes upon them. Alexander is a person who had the range of expressing himself, like in Saks Fifth Avenue and Bloomingdale's perhaps, where Rico wouldn't go, or Bobby Foster wouldn't even think of going. So there are differences in that. Alexander is a man who was bred out of a Black elegance, and Foster's a street dude, and Rico is another kind of con man.

Bob: How did you happen to get involved in theater, or acting?

Dick: That's very deep, you see, because when I was a teenager, people would say, what are you going to wind up doing? I would say I didn't know, but I could tell you several things that I wasn't going to do, and the top was always, ACT. 'Cause I didn't like to be around actors. I didn't like people who talked about themselves, or the games that actors play, or the things that they try out on you. I didn't understand

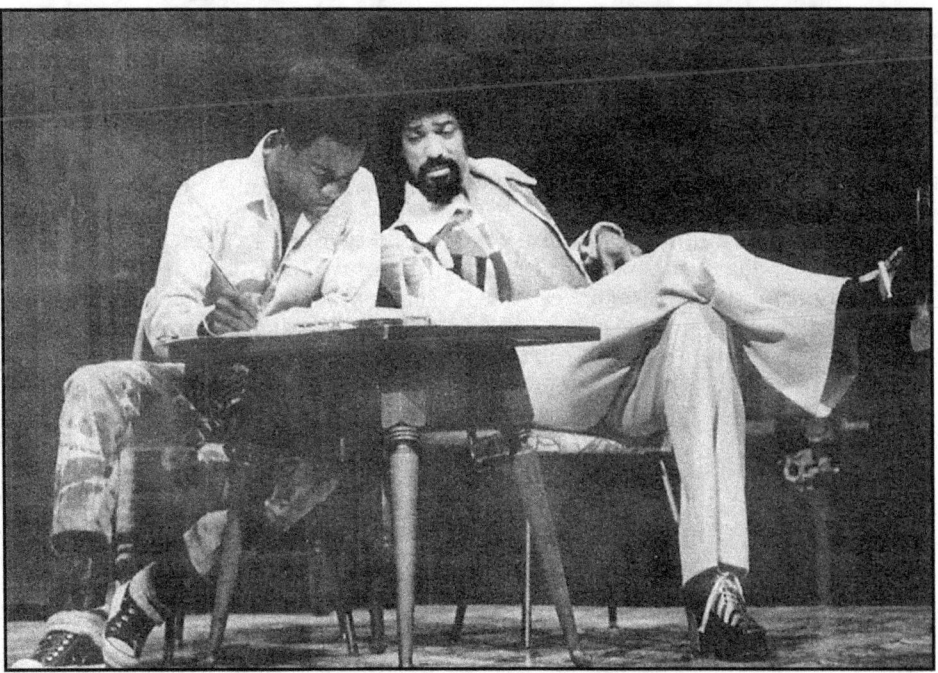

Glynn Turman and Dick A. Williams in *What the Wine Sellers Buy.*

actors at all. So I said, that is one unreal, gaudy place that I don't want to go. I felt that most of the dudes who were into acting were, y'know. . .strange, and it went against my gang values, my street values. I came up in Chicago. How I got into acting, I don't know. I was a painter, and I had won some little scholarships. I went through a whole lot of things. I had polio and I went to a school for crippled children for three years (Spaldings School in Chicago). I even body-guarded for a little while; I did a lot of different things. I was also a poet around Chicago.

Bob: What are some of the things that you would like to see presented in the theatre, and what do you think that people should start thinking about?

Dick: I don't know what that thing is, but the searching is the thing that I think is a gas. What I'd like to see happen in the theatre? The most paramount thing that Black people should start thinking about right now, that I can think of, is the potential heroes that we've lost and alienated; all the Black greatness that we call passe. We don't give any credit to the people that we call Uncle Toms; we negate their whole existence, while the white race call these people heroes. I mean, Laurel and Hardy are heroes; I mean, they are great people. Bud Abbott and Lou Costello are great people. Look at the white comedians that are brilliant, brilliant. But then Stepin Fetchit is a TOM? All the Amos and Andy people are TOMS? I mean, right down the list, there are Black comedians who are TOMS, who people call TOMS. Maybe not the current ones, not now, but we don't know what will happen five years from now. You take Jackie Robinson in baseball; I've heard him called a TOM. That's ridiculous! Babe Ruth is a great hero? Right now, Hank Aaron is cool, but what will we do with him? Jack Dempsey's a great fighter; Joe Louis is a TOM?

Bob: Why do you think that is? Why do people do that?

Dick: For one, I think it's because we don't really believe that we are beautiful. Beyond all the Black and Beautiful rhetoric, that comes out. I don't think that we really think that we are beautiful. We can't laugh at ourselves, there's no black comedy. That's the kind of uptightness that we need to transcend. I think it's easier for us to fight each other than to deal with more important problems. See, I think, in a way, that whole battle of Black/White relationships is unimportant. Man constantly aspires to be more than that. He will not accept his position in the universe. I think that man aspires to be a god and creates gods in his image. If man

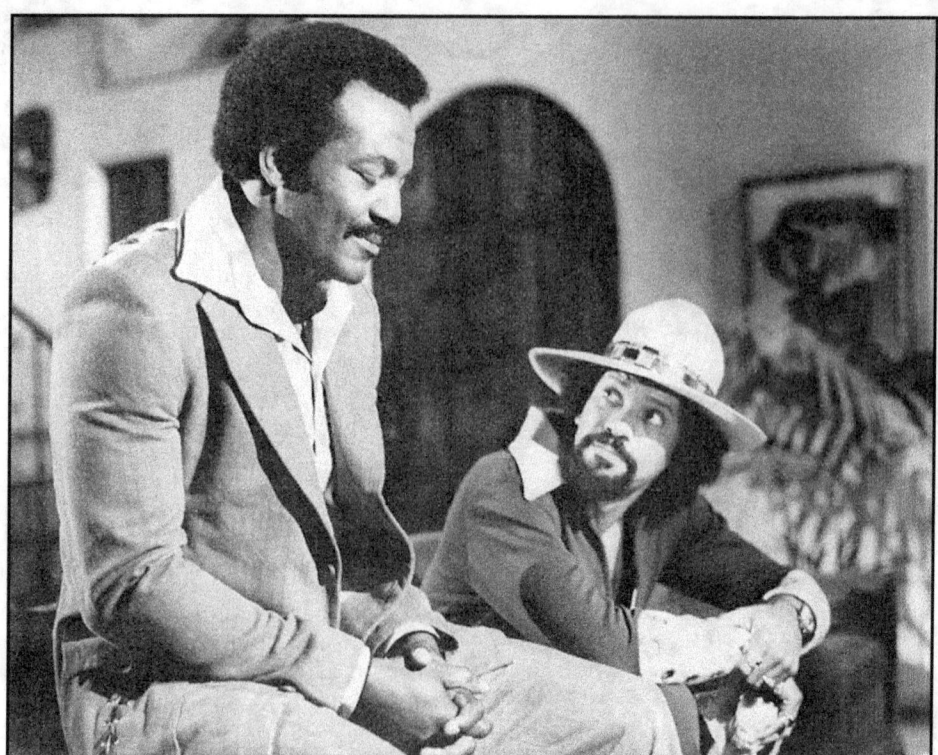

Jim Brown and Dick A. Williams in *Slaughter's Big Rip-Off.*

accepted where he was, I think it would be a much better world. We know very little about life, about death, about birth and cancer; about what we are all about, and where we're going. We really know absolutely nothing about that. So I think that the energy, and frustration of dealing with thousands and thousands of men's thinking hasn't been able to come up with a suitable answer for everybody. It's such an insurmountable thing that the frustration is turned inward. The Orientals have a very beautiful philosophy. Instead of trying to pull out of what we know of as the universe, as something very special, they join it. They are willing to become a drop of water, thereby becoming part of the whole universe. A man did not make the whole universe as we know it: Neptune, Jupiter, the stars, the other universes. I don't think that man, with his abilities, could have made it. Yet man would pretend to be king of all this.

Bob: What do you think about the comment that violence on the screen has a definite relationship to the increase in violence in the society at large?

Dick: I don't agree that violence on the T.V. provokes violence in the street. I think that this nation was conceived very violently. That was before T.V., and before movies. I think that one of the reasons that we are such an insane nation is because no one acknowledges what happens to the Black man in this nation. No one acknowledges what happens to the Indians here. No one acknowledges what happens to all the minorities that come in here. We

pretend as if that does not happen, and we go on. I think that the truth need be told. I think that the only way that there will be an American theatre is when the theatre begins to reflect what's happening. You walk into a Broadway theatre, and you look on stage, and up to most recently everybody was white. . .except a Black carrying a tray, or with a chauffeur's cap. But then you can walk out into the street and see black, white, yellow, brown, red, and so forth. We've taken our theatre from the English, theatre, which I think is bad because we have not really created an indigenous American theatre. Every piece that comes out and tries to reflect what's happening out here gets killed right away. Mainly, this is because it doesn't fall into some value system that the English theatre or the Russian theatre or the German theatre created, and that this country draws on. It's not really about creating it s own theatre, and it should be about that. For instance, I don't even like to talk too much about Black Exploitation Pictures. At first I thought, "Yeah", but I've done a lot of thinking about it. See, all of a sudden, when COTTON COMES TO HARLEM, SHAFT and SWEETBACK came out, BAM, white people realized that there are Black people who pay money to see films. They saw that these things were making millions of dollars, that people were paying millions of dollars to see them. There **is** a Black audience. But the thing is that the Black audience wasn't created with those things; they were already there. I mean, I was a part

Cont'd on page 49

actor, where four days after the opening, it closed. I've never had that experience, and it's a little strange. I've had an interesting career in which most of the plays, not all of them, have always ran. The shortest were the two plays that I did Off-Broadway that ran about two weeks after the opening, and that's because they didn't have any back-up money to keep them going. Which is the problem with this play. This play is not an unsuccessful play, and I don't think that the critics really killed the play. I think that any time you bring any play any place, you should plan it with a loss and have money accordingly, for at least two or three weeks, in order to build your audience size.

Bob: Four days, I just can't see that anyway. . .

Cleavon: Well, one of the problems we had was, when we were out of town, we didn't make the kind of money necessary. . .they lost money. And so, when we came in town. . .we almost didn't open the play, but they raised enough money to be able to do it until the end of this week. Then after that it was hoped that the reviews would be very good and substantial. . .

Bob: It was a gamble. . .

Cleavon: Yeah.

Bob: This particular character (Willie Stepp) represents a different kind of role for you in a way. Was it a different kind of experience for you, and how so?

Cleavon: I think more than for me, it was a different kind of experience for audiences that have seen me act. I've done other serious things, but nothing of this magnitude, because they weren't brought to Broadway. However, I haven't done a lot of serious things for, I guess, the past four or five years, that were like this. I've done a couple of television things. But to do a play with the actors that are in this play, and they're all very fine actors, and to work on it over a period of seven or eight, ten weeks, was very important, and it was an important growth. It was sort of a culmination of a lot of things that I know about acting, and being able to put it all in this character. The character is funny, but he's not funny. He says something very important, and sometimes he says things that aren't important. He has his own emotional feelings that range from very high to very low, which is an interesting character for me to play. The growth of working in a company like this, and seeing some of the problems we as actors have and had with the script, was an important growth. So that I feel I'm ready to do another play—a serious play, not necessarily a comedy, but I would like to do another drama, to expand even

more. Acting, to me, is a way of growing, spiritually, emotionally, and psychologically, but only as long as you keep it in perspective. I don't mean that you act when you're off-stage, but I mean the working process of learning about the character, and about the play, and the playwright, and the director, and that's where I think personal growth comes in. I feel good about that.

Bob: How does getting into a character help these things to happen?

Cleavon: It's certainly true in this play that each character in this play represents a part of each of us. There are times for all Black people—and I make very few exceptions—when we believe very strongly in some of the things that Willie Stepp talks about. . . his philosophies and where his head is. He just thinks. There are times when we are all very emotional, as Bobby Foster is, and not think about something but really feel. There are times when we all, under certain circumstances, are very Uncle Tommish, like Hurspool. And I think anybody who says that they're not, is only lying to themselves. We can give it another title. . .we can give it a title of compromise over something else that we want that's greater. Even the most militant get in that position; it's a negotiating position. And that's what this country is basically run by: a negotiation for one thing or another. There are times when some of us just trip out,like Charles Jefferson(played by Northern Calloway) when we're at out wit's end and we're very irrational; we'll hang ourselves. So for that reason, for me to see the play from that point of view, and for anybody who comes to see the play, if you really think about it and can identify with it, you know that there are a lot of parts of you as a human being that make you function. A lot of times we as human beings only function in the most safe, secure way, and we don't want to do anything that goes beyond that. All we want is a house in the suburbs, and a car, and to go to work, come home, and watch television, and that's secure. And anybody who confronts that security, with some idea of protesting against unrighteousness, threatens our security. So for me that play has just presented it much more intensely, of which I'm quite happy. That is a kind of growth that makes me more secure; to know that there is a lot of insecurity, which is easier to deal with, when you don't live in a false world.

Cal Wilson: Do you feel that you are more a comic actor or a comedian? Do you feel that you could be a stand-up comedian?

Cleavon: I've never done stand-up comedy. It would scare the Hell out of

me. I'm not a comic actor. I am first an actor who can do tragedy, and can do comedy, can do satire, can do anything that's called upon me to do as an actor. Now, what has happened in my own career is that the things that have taken me to any point of recognition have been comedy things. If I should get exposed to doing some dramatic things, I can go there, too. I haven't had that opportunity; I haven't had those kinds of scripts that have been written and produced, where somebody said we're gonna do this and we want you to do it. That experience rarely has happened; it's happen in this case, and that's why I'm doing it.

Cal: Then it's not that you've had a particular preference for comedy in the past?

Cleavon: No. The first play I ever did in New York was a play called **Mac Bird**. A small part, but it happened to be a funny part. And it was a big hit. No one offered me anything. . .I was offered **Does a Tiger Wear A Necktie**? during the summer, and that was a serious part. He was a heavy cat, and I did that. No one knows about that, because that was out of the city. The next part that I got was for a play called **Scuba Duba**, and it was a comedy part. I was learning, growing as an actor, and it was very funny and it was a big hit. So what can you do? I've done some things Off-Broadway that were serious and they didn't go well. . .not because of the acting but because of the fact that they were poorly produced at the time, and that's why they didn't continue. So I see myself very strongly as an actor.

Cal: What kind of impact do you think **Blazing Saddles** has had on your career in terms of possibly locking people into identifying with you as that type of character?

Cleavon: **Blazing Saddles** is Mel Brooks. Most people who see me say they saw **Blazing Saddles** and they thought it was very funny. The industry, I think sees it in that respect. If it had any impact that was significant, I would probably be working as a movie actor constantly. In fact I have not done a film in two and a half, maybe three years. I've had no offers to do any substantial role. I have had offers to do some things that I didn't do because they weren't what I wanted to do, but very few.

Bob: What kind of character would you like to play?

Cleavon: That's always a hard question for me to answer. The character that I'm doing is one kind of character; I think he's a character of ideas, and good ideas. But I'd like to do a character that is dealing in a situation that is real. An important example would be to do a show about a man who has a family, and how he has to live with his family; the problems that he has with having a family; the problems that he has with society; the problems that he may have with himself. A man who has anxieties and fears and frustrations; a man who's able to laugh and to cry, a real man, a total man, a really human being. Not a one-dimensional man who's operating from a one-dimensional frame, but a real, well-rounded person. He may be an unhealthy man, he could be crazy, I don't mind that, but something that has some substance. It's hard to pin point that, because then you're talking about a script. And that's another thing, you see. Those are very hard for a lot of actors to get. Most white actors get those availed to them, but Black actors don't get that opportunity too much because most of the movies we get are so-called exploitation films. I don't even like that term because I'm not necessarily anti-exploitation film. I think that all films are exploitation films; it's only become intensified because it's black people who are seing the films. I would love to do a gangster movie. Paul Newman does it, Robert Redford, they all do it. The problem with what happens with us is, we get the athletes who get all those great movies, and unfortunately they can't act, in my opinion, and they become exploitation movies. Some of the athletes exploit those by producing and directing that kind of movie, and not really getting involved with actors who are from New York or from Los Angeles, who are serious, and have studied for years. They do a lot of movies that I would not mind doing. There are some movies so-called Black exploitation movies that I would do. They would not be as exploitive as they are, because I certainly would argue for some legitimacy in those films, in making them good, not just C or D exploitation movies. I'm not against exploitation movies. But there are exploitation movies that are A exploitation movies. I'm not against that. As long as it's well-produced, well written and well directed. When I was in Chicago I went to see a movie, and I rarely go to movies. It was in the loop in Chicago; which it's predominately Black people are in that area of the city at night—It was called "Killer Elite", with James Caan and Robert Duvall, who are former stage actors, who are movie actors, who are stars. The whole theater was packed with Black people. That same movie, you could have changed the characters and made them Black, and it's an exploitation movie. I should be able to do the same kind of movie, and do it as a character. I would love to do a character and put a patch over my eye, and give him a beard, and make his

head bald, and give him a little limp, something like that. He's a bad dude! That's not my personality; I'm tired of giving from that.

Bob: What motivated you to become involved in theater?

Cleavon: Well, I started in high school studying acting. That was 1957. I had a teacher from a kind of an old school. A white teacher, who taught acting from a basic concept. Then I learned history of theater; then I went on through college and studied acting. Acting to me is an art; it's not just something I do as a living, and it's not something I just all of a sudden decided, I'm going to be an actor. We have a lot of young Black actors who say "I want to be an actor," come up to me, "I want to go to Hollywood," and "I want to get in the movies," and that's bullshit. To me, if I'm going to be a football player, I've got to work out and get my body in shape and learn how to play it and be prepared for it. As an actor I do that by working on the stage and constantly coming back, so if I do a film. . . There are a couple of good projects coming up, good characters, it will be something. It will be something people will have to take note of. And that's why I'd rather take the time. But I love that, and it is an important thing and I don't take it lightly. The motivation is just something that I like to do. It's like, if you're a writer and you like to write, you're gonna write at what you like to. You may at times write in areas because you have to make a living, but if you really are serious about it, you also are doing something that is significant to you.

Cal: Would you like to do another musical?

Cleavon: Sure. But I don't want to do a musical that comes out of a book or something else. I want to do an original musical with original, interesting characters. . .that I would like to do and with talented people. So I would do another musical.

Bob: This is really a silly question but are you impressed with being Cleavon Little?

Cleavon: No, I'm impressed with being the son of Malachi Little and (unclear—mother's name) Little. I think that's a trip.

Bob: How do you respond when people see and approach you in the street?

Cleavon: I really don't pay too much attention to that. I'm really interested in seeing who that person is and knowing who they are and how they're affected. If they in fact come on without really seeing anything, then I tend to just say hello and give them an autograph and go about my business. I figure there's a danger in becoming impressed with yourself, because you stop being your-

self. You start becoming an image, a mirror of yourself, and once you do that, you no longer can act. I just don't deal with it. Cleavon Little that's my name, that's what I was born with, that's who I am, that's just part of my identity. But it's kind of a trip, I've thought about it on occasion, just sat down and said to myself, "I'm Cleavon Little," and I did this, I won this, and I've done that, and that's all I could think of and I would not take it any further, because it would be a lot of other bullshit things. You'd expect certain treatment because you are who you are. I don't expect anything more for me than I do for you, or for you. We still get up in the morning and we go to the bathroom and we eat food and we do the same things.

Bob: Haven't the awards affected you?

Cleavon: No, I don't think so. I don't pay too much attention to them. I appreciate them because they show that somebody appreciates what I've done, and that's it. There are other priorities more important to me in my life.

Cal: Had you had a lot of singing and dancing experience before **Purlie**?

Cleavon: No. (laughs) When I did **Purlie** I was scared to death. I didn't want to do it, in fact, because I'm not a singer, and there were some professional singers in **Purlie** that could SING. Nor do I dance. I've worked at it; I've taken classes in movement, and I know how to move, and even when I was going through school I did some things that would afford me to try to sing, but it has always been a very frightening thing. Finally, for me to do **Purlie** was more of a challenge to try to master being able to sing in front of an audience, because it had always made me nervous, and to get over that fear as a performer. Which I think I've partially done. I haven't done enough musicals to have done it to my satisfaction, and I should take classes in singing. And whenever I get some time, that's what I will do. It was more of a challenge to do **Purlie** than it was to do really, anything.

Bob: Is there anything else concerning the stage work that you have anxiety about, that you would like to overcome so that you can grow?

Cleavon: No, other than that I would love to do a good character part, an old man. I'd love that. I love the thought of trying to do that. Not necessarily an old man that starts old, but one that starts younger and moves to that point. The other thing is that there are no anxieties that I have; there are only challenges. I am still just beginning to move into the area of doing some serious things, and I want to investigate that more, either on film or television or on stage. I just feel at this stage that I want to move into that more. I don't intend to go back into doing comedy. I would do comedy now because I've been away from it for a little while. I don't intend to really make that my forte, unless somebody offered me a great film that happened to be funny. I certainly would do that.

Bob: Are you interested in producing, directing. . .what happens behind the scenes?

Cleavon: Yes, I am. I've given myself a time for all of those things. I would like to get involved in directing in about four or five years, specifically film, but there's some things I want to learn about that in terms of the camera. Producing, that's interesting, but I don't know if I want to do that. That entails another kind of position, and that's not necessarily a creative position, for me. So I'll just wait and see. I'm not rushing anything. I'm still excited about acting.

Cal: One of the serious roles you had that I remember was in **Vanishing Point**. You played a blind disc jockey. What kind of experience was that?

Cleavon: That was one of my favorite film experieces. It's hard to say what kind of experience it was; it was on in which the character was serious, and at that time I think it was a very important project to be done. The film didn't do well here but it did very well in Europe. It made a lot of money, which I wish I could have gotten some of. But it was probably one of my best experiences, because he was a blind disc jockey. It was a good character role.

Bob: Do you consider yourself a funny man?

Cleavon: You mean in film or. . . .

Bob: In real life.

Cleavon: I don't, but people I know do. (laughter) People are always telling me that. One of my friends, Dick Williams, always says to me, "You're funny." And I don't know why, because he's the one that's funny. Dick, if you know him, has this kind of tall, stately, "Right on, Brother" look to him, and I have had more fun with him in doing this play. . . He's like a little bitty kid. He comes into my dressing room and looks at me and tries to steal something out of here, and we play like two little boys, two little bad boys. And he's funny! Now that is a funny nigguh! But he thinks I'm funny. So we all have those funny things about us. It's hard to say. I think I have a sense of humor that has to be captured, but for me to say, "Well, I'm gonna be funny". . .

Bob: Academicians talk about the roots of creativity. There's been one theory that to be truly creative, one has to be in touch with that childlike nature inside themselves. How do you respond to your creativity?

Cleavon: I think that's true. I think you have to be open with that part of yourself to be creative, just to see things from a lot of points of view. We as adults become very sophisticated, supposedly, in how we see things; kids see things from all kinds of angles. A kid would come into this room and see these walls and want to know what this is all about. We'll just come in and accept it as it is. I think that all the discussion on creative processes have truth in them. I don't know which is my truth except that I would like to think that from a little bit of all of it, I have that experience. And I certainly have found out that I'm more highly evolved and creative now, after having a marriage and going through a lot of emotional changes that had their positive and negative aspects, and it's over. But it certainly forced me to touch some emotions that I never did before, and I can only say that that experience has made me much more creative, and much freer. ✿

D.A. WILLIAMS
Cont'd from page 46
of that audience, 'cause as a kid I was watching Tarzan and Hoot Gibson and all those old jive turkeys. . .now, look at the violence in those exploitation things. So it's not just something that just happened. My head is full of Tarzan and full of all those old World War II flight pictures; full of musicals, full of all that junk that they've been throwing down. I don't see anything wrong with a SHAFT. SHAFT is no more or less a fantasy than James Bond is, and I haven't heard one Black person saying one thing about James Bond. Black people went and saw some JAMES BOND! I mean, there a lot of Blacks who will brag to you, telling you that they have seen every JAMES BOND picture that has come out. They'll tell you how

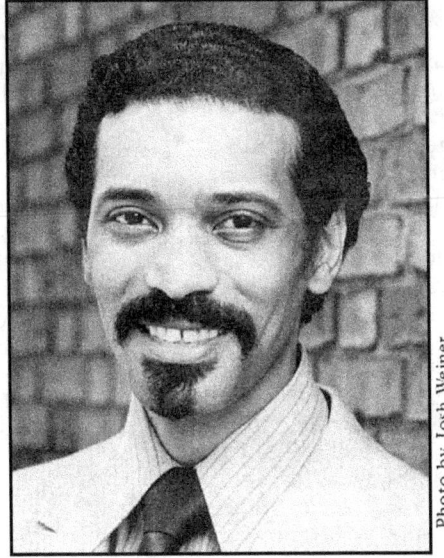

Photo by Josh Weiner

bad the dude is. So there's nothing wrong with, instead of it being Sean Connery, that it's Jim Brown or Richard Roundtree or Max Julien or Ron O'Neal. I don't really see that. I think that there's a weight that we put on people that is really not theirs.

Bob: Then we have to talk about producing?

Dick: That's where you've got to go. That's what you've got to do. The producer, the distributor, that's the root of the whole thing. If me and you make a film and we put everything we got in it and we get a canned product, we have to have someplace to show that product. That's when you run into a brother producer and a brother distributor, who can take 65%, and you take 35%. All that he's providng is the house. That can happen. You've got to run into that, and those are the people who make the decisions, because you're not going to make a product that ain't going to sell. It's like, you know, grants limit people when they get 'em, not because the people who give the money say, you better not do this, you better not do that, or tell you what to do. It's becasue they say, write me a proposal and tell me what you're going to do. Well, you're going to consider the person who you're writing the proposal to, and you're going to design the proposal along those lines, and you are editing yourself.

Bob: As an actor, how do you approach your craft?

Dick: As an actor, you have to be able to see through the cat's eyes and accept his reality. You have to accept the reality of the character. When you find a person unable to identify with a character, there is usually a refusal to accept the identity of the character. Sometimes it happens where a writer doesn't go in and reveal himself; he won't take his things off. Usually if you can accept the circumstances of a play or the circumstance of the character, you can identify with the character. I'm not playing Dick Williams. I haven't done that yet. I use Dick Williams. I use my experiences, and I don't believe in emotional recall. Where I come from is that I try to make the situation real for me within the framework of what's laid down by the writer. *There's* a tremendous amount of latitude, y'know. If you accept it, automatically you begin to have emotional responses to things, the more you accept it. Of course, maybe, there's an overall sense of structure in me, where I'm continually aware of the overall thing in a play. But most importantly, don't lie to yourself. Most people can't look at themselves in the mirror; that's a mind-blowing experience for most people. Be honest with yourself. ✿

rush to get to his aunt's house. This characteristically verbose "Leo" hadn't very much to say. They stood up on the "F" train. He took out English cherry gumdrops, and pressed one into her mouth. He was so real! She loved candy; the sweeter it was, the more she wanted. She could not collect her thoughts. She did not know what they had talked about, but he had told her, when they first met, that his office was in the process of moving, as he was a Black businessman of midtown Manhattan. She was delighted to have a man of such importance at her side. The ride home on the bus was a joy. She had asked him to be very polite to her mother; he said that he would be.

"This is Bill!" she said to her mother as they entered the door to the apartment on Christopher Street. Her mother said hello, and Bill greeted her cordially. Kay was impressed. Marilyn and Bill sat down in the living room to have tea. After bringing him his tea, Marilyn touched him. He stood her up and kissed her, sweetly. "Lord!" she thought to herself. "Can he kiss!" His lips were as soft as her lips in the most special place. His tasted like honey.

He pulled her by the hand into her bedroom. She unzipped his pants, but he had long-johns on. Oh! The seconds were precious but time-consuming. He got himself out, and asked her to love him. She told him that she couldn't. God! Was he disappointed. So was she. Marilyn had never intended to refuse him. Everything had happened so fast. She told him her problem. He told her that she must see a doctor, and she promised him that she would. She had been afraid, afraid that she had cancer. She had believed that no one cared, and that she would have to face the problem alone.

They went back to the living room. Her mother had remained in the kitched, cooking, even after Marilyn had stepped into her cup of tea, which sat on the floor, and even afer it had spilled out on the carpet, and even while she and Bill were in her room. Then, in walked Anna with Hassen Ali. As Marilyn had told almost everyone about Bill, Anna and Hassen knew as much about him as she did. They sat discussing cars, as Anna drove a Volvo, and Bill had owned an old Mercedes-Benz. They concluded their conversation with talk about leadership, and Black national leaders. After they had argued the point beyond recognizable proportions, Bill decided that he had to leave, as his aunt was expecting him. Anna and Hassen had not hit it off well wtih Bill.

The descending elevator ride was lovely. Marilyn kissed him again. She tired to walk him to the bus stop, but he asked her to return home. He ran the remainder of the distance for the bus. When he got on, he stopped to ask something of the driver; he then proceded to the back of the bus. She speculated that he must not have the carefare, after paying her way on the bus earlier that afternoon. But she could only guess, because she never heard from him, or saw him, again.

While he was in her house, she had gotten him to give her another of his phoney, dead-end numbers, this time an address. The first time he had disappeared, Bill had given her a telephone number to call, which turned out to belong to an advertising agency. She went over to the street on which he had claimed to live, only to find that there was no such address on the entire block. Yes, Bill was gone, FOREVER!

She attended summer school at Hunter. Again, she took only one subject, Typing II. She got an "A". One of Anna's friends happened to be visiting her one even-

ing—Joe, of the Persuasions, an acappella singing group. He asked her why she didn't try to attend New York Community College, where she could matriculate with nine credits. She decided to inquire at the college. Marilyn went over to admissions; she entered that fall. After she had gained nine credits, she transferred to day school.

Even at Hunter she had found that trying to acquire a college education at her age was a sacrifice, but it was worse at Community. She had found it a miserable experience, a futile, never-ending struggle. Marilyn rushed out to school daily, and on time, only to rush home on time. None of the men attending the school ever paid very much attention to her. She had hoped to fall in love and get married. The men who did give her a moment, or two, wanted her to spend both her time and her money. She was determined to avoid this "plan" in the future.

While marriage had been a "social" question when she was sixteen, it had become "political" by the time she had reached 26, but she no longer cared if a man had money or not. A place in his life was all that she wanted, as no Black man was poor to her, after Bill.

Although she had decided that Bill Harriston had probably been a "hustler," or a male prostitute, or even a "pimp," she believed that she would always love him for coming to her, and for going after her. It had been many years since a man had shown her such attention.

Still, she would have gone to pieces if she had not had a secret lover. Yes, he was how she had gotten over. The disappointments, which she had already encountered on whatever avenue she walked, would have driven a moron wild. Everywhere, a lousy end! The man whom she loved had given her the belief in herself that she could live a normal life, expecting the things that any other woman her age expected, regardless of Fate. He was every man that she could ever love. Yet, she loved him to betroth, and he was the only husband that she would ever know in her heart, mind, and soul. She had fallen in love with him when she was sixteen-and-a-half. She believed then that they would never meet, but really, like a woman would believe, she knew that they would, even though she could not imagine when, or where. They met when she was twenty-four; at that time he was thirty-one. You see, he was a very famous star, even when she was a teenager.

Johnny Memphis was a Handsome millionaire, and as she had then written, "the philosopher of her dreams." He had always been a wonderful, brilliant "boy," and time could never take his youthfulness away from him. He was a magnificent dream-come-true, but the near she came to him, the further away he would go. From the time that they met, to love him had been a nightmare. She could never touch him, or make love to him, but only call to him as she believed he had called to her for so many years. He was the man she had hoped to meet when she was yet a child, the boy whom she was destined to meet, the one about whom she had dreamed, until she no longer believed herself logical. She had waited for him, throwing all realities aside.

After learning that she would probably never hold him in her arms, Marilyn's mind collapsed on three separate occasions. Every time she would regain her senses, she would have a relapse. It was just too difficult for her, but she decided that she would never give him up. After a forth time in the hospital, she decided that it was her last, that even though he could not kiss her eyes, or hold her hands to his body, he was "alive and well!" So, she would be likewise. No, he would probably never take her out to dine, or to dance, but she had seen each dream of her youth fall apart, and she knew that she must continue to live with the mind-splitting tremors, the soul-shattering realities, the hard fact that she had always loved dreams, and had lived nightmares, and would continue to do so for the rest of her life. No! She could not have the obscene dislikes or likes that the average woman has, as she would be spoken of as paranoid, but she believed that it would suffice to someday be able to tell her husband, and their children, how she got over, and she was preparing herself for them, and that day. ✿

BARBARA ANN TEER *Cont'd from page* 18

I plan to take a piece on a national tour. Also, I plan to eventually take a piece to Broadway or to a house that is considered legitimate in the Western sense. That may be a Lincoln Center, or Broadway; a place that can seat a large amount of people. It will take a large amount of money. Our home is Harlem; we love our location on Fifth Avenue, but we need more office space. We find that people are frightened of coming to Harlem. When we want to reach more than 150 people, we have to go outside of our home. We want to create a profitable touring program. Our overall goal is for the National Black Theater to become a highly visible institution so that we can reach more people, and grow, and expand. Also, so that we can afford to present quality workshops, quality productions, and quality special events. The overall direction that NBT is going in, is this: I would like to set up, for the first time in history, a Master of Black Arts University. There are none in the world; even in Africa, the institutions have European bases. They don't teach their own culture. I would like to have a university on Black Arts, based on an African or an African-American experience. And in order to do that, which is a major job, we must first conduct projects, like performing. So we can get the kind of visibility we need. People —and places like the University of Michigan, Vassar, Sarah Lawrence— have called us to ask if they could study with us as a field project. They get tremendous satisfaction out of it, but we would like to expand it so that we could become the accredited university.

How did you evolve the theory of acting that you use in NBT?

I think I answered that in the first question when I talked about the standard. I went to five universities in America, studying dance and drama, and I studied in Europe for six months. When I came back, I studied at the Henry Street Playhouse for three years with Alan Nikolai. I really got to experience myself mastering European techniques of theater, as far as the performing aspect of it, and then I hurt my knee one night, and I had to stop dancing for six months. I started seriously studying acting. I studied with the best acting teachers there were in the West at that time: Sanford Musner—I was with him for six years on and off; Phillip Burton, studying Shakespeare. At a point, all my teachers got together and said, "Barbara, you don't need to study anymore. You really have mastered this technique, go and work". And there was no place to work. When I auditioned for parts, the only roles were for maids and prostitutes, and I said, well, when I get old I can look

forward to being a matriarch. Those one-dimensional parts were all that were offered to me. And I had all this technique. So I took it out and put it internally and that's how I came up with what I did.

What are the dynamics of the NBT acting technique?

I don't like that word "acting," you know. That's why I avoided it. In the early Sixties, I took all my acting techniques and started a group called Group Theater Workshop with Robert Hooks. And I really discovered by working with teenagers, . . .by the way, the Group Theater Workshop is the original Negro Ensemble Company; it started from the Group Theater Workshop, and I really would like to credit myself for having begun the Negro Ensemble Company. And you can compare the difference, becasue the Negro Ensemble Company is an acting company and the NBT has taken a totally different direction. I moved away from the concepts of acting, because they come out of a base that says that there's something outside that one must strive to become. I do a lot of solo lectures, and the topic of the lectures is "From Self-Conscious Art To God-Conscious Art." And self-conscious art is acting. You have to study a lot of different kinds of disciplines; twenty types of dance. All of it to take you to a space where you can perform. It makes you tremendously self-conscious; no matter how much technique you get, it's never enough. You're insecure, you're always nervous, every job is a first job. Every job, you wait for the reviews to evaluate you to tell you if you're good enough to apply for another job. And it's vicious cycle. It's not a very happy existence, because you live in the fear of someone else continually evaluating you. What I discovered was that theater is not that, for me, because that comes out of a Western standard. So we are liberators and communicators—you don't have one discipline, you are everything. The people in NBT, as liberator, communicator, are in fact administrators, musicians, technicians; they can sing, dance, act—they can do everything, becasue life is about everything. It's not about separating; it's about things being inter-related, because who you are is God. And if you're God, everything flows from you that particular reference point. That means you can do anything, or whatever is necessary to get the job done, and the job is to totally liberate your mind, and your spirit. Set your spirit free. So, therefore, the technique that I have evolved is one that I think would totally turn the thrust of Western theater around. And that's why I would like the company to be more fully exposed, because then people could see the end result of this training.

When one participates in the NBT experience, is the experience spontaneous?

You'd have to ask the people who go through the experience. I don't know.

Is the ritual rehearsed?

Oh, no, that's years of technique, that's the point. I'm not going to write a book about how I train liberators. You see, that's scientific. It's a way of dealing with space. You know, jazz musicians start out with improvisation and sometimes they never put it into a form. Africans are improvisational, experimental. They don't come from form to experience; they go from experience to form. That's what we do, you know. It looks spontaneous; the science is to make it look spontaneous. It's very set. That's part of the whole technique. The only thing that's not set is what the people do in the audience, who we call participants. We can't judge that. Some nights when it's really cooking we go on forever and ever—we may be there for four or five hours. Because the participants are out there doing their thing. Some nights, if nobody wants to join in, it may be an hour and a half or two hours.

Your use of "preacher rhythms" seems to be similar to the "testifying" found in the church.

I don't like the word "testifying", because if you're sharing experience, that's just what you're doing. sharing an experience. If you're testifying —and I don't know the definition of testifying— it seems that you're trying to validate something that's been put out there. Nothing is put out there; all we ask them to do is close their eyes and whatever they get, they get. And because they are so excited about what they got, they want to share it. It has nothing to do with anything except that they got to experience certain relationships in their lives and they wanted to share it with the family. It's like when you see something so great that you can't wait to tell your friend about it because you love your friend and you want him to experience what you experienced. You say, hey, man, go see that, it's dynamite. That's not testifying; I call it sharing.

how do you feel about social reform programs and government aid—what some people would call government hand-outs?

Well, I don't know about government hand-outs. My point is that as long as Black people experience themselves as oppressed, they will be looking for help, for hand-outs. Many Black people experience themselves as victims, and I am not a victim. As long as you buy the lie, then something is wrong. And you need help; that means something is wrong. If you feel that you don't have what somebody else has, you come out of what we call the have-nots. There's the have-nots and the haves; the haves experience themselves as getting what they want, having want they want, being what they want. And there are people who've experienced just the opposite; they are hostile and full of hatred, and are full of negative thought, and they blame it on things outside themselves. It's not healthy for your own personal instrument to have those kinds of thoughts. Because the instrument is a divine house, this body, and when you're upset it causes diseases of all kinds. What I'm saying is much larger than the government and all that. When Black people start experiencing from the having-ness of what they are, from the I-am-ness of who they are, what happens is, they might look for assistance but not for help. It's just the difference in those two words. People have to stay in touch with survival. Because we're going to survive; nothing is going to keep us from surviving. We just have to be more creative and more inventive, and figure out ways to do for ourselves. I'm about developing people who are self-motivated and self-determined, not people who are looking for hand-me-downs and begging and getting mad because this great white man up here won't give me what I ask him for, so I'm going to picket around his block. That doesn't turn me on. For the people that it turns on, that's really all right, right on. But I don't beg, because I understand who I am. And when you're clear who you are, you come the space of being who you are. You don't have to beg; you just simply say, this is a great

idea, would you like to assist me in making it happen. If the man says yes, you say right on; if he says no, you still say right on, because that is not going to stop the idea from happening.

To what principle element do you attribute the success and longevity of the NBT?

Self-love. If you look on our brochure, you will see a mantra. We call it a Black mantra. We got it a year ago, from a brother; I really can't remember his name. It says: *I Got To Love Myself So Much, That I Can Love You So Much, That You Can Love You So Much, That You Can Start Loving Me.* That's really what it's all about. In the opening song to the revival, it says, there's a science to living, there's a science to loving, there's a science to holding a hand, there's a science to giving, there's a science to caring. And it goes on and on. You see, in this country there's a science to taking a ship to the moon, and to math and culture, but you very rarely hear talk about a science to loving. So much so that people don't want to use the word "love" because it sounds corny. That's all a part of the master plan. There have to be schools designed to train people to love themselves, just as there are schools to train people to deal with mathematics. And the original place where that was to happen was the church. Not the church as a building, but the institution called religion. So that in the East you have more emphasis on meditation of Man, Voodoo, Yoruba. That's where it starts. But here, where it starts is in the money world, the political world, and there's a whole element of humanism that's never dealt with. We are interested in developing human beings; expanding the consciousness of human beings so that they can experience themselves as perfect. We are not interested in the other self.   So when you ask me what the element is, we

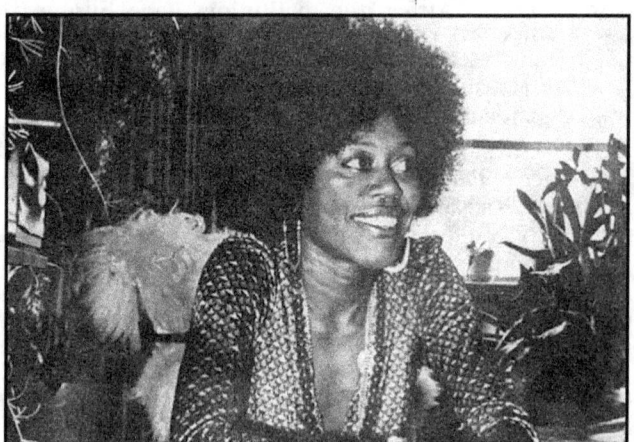

call it love. What love is, is energy, and who you are is energy, and who I am is energy, and who God is is energy. It's not masculine or feminine; it's both. It's not some little god up in the sky who doesn't have any time for us because he's so transcendental. God is sitting right here in this chair talking to you and responding to me. There's a god within and a god without, and together with God we can straighten all this stuff out. Our job is to refine and experience who we are so that we can all experience our perfection. And so what I'm really talking about is how to find and perfect your own energy system so that it works for you as opposed to you working for it. —**C.W.** ✿

The National Black Theater is located at 9 East 125th Street, New York City.

OTIS AND DANCE

Cont'd from page 7

and his ability to express the human drama.

Otis' drama is as untraditional as his choreography. The Lincoln Housing Project was the backdrop of Sallid's early expression. The usual stories of ultra-violence and social agony didn't inhibit the choreograher's growing up. The incidents were definitely there: the Lincoln projects in the early sixtites; nine-year-old, marauding rip-off artists; the dope dealers and the rest of the insanity that characterized low-income living during that period. Sallid's inclination towards the arts, however, took him past all that into a federally-funded arts and culture center and his first dance lesson.

After Performing Arts High School, Julliard, and a host of good teachers, Sallid decided not to join a major company. He spent time doing odd jobs and seeing what life was about. Says Otis, "I had to do a lot of things to survive. I sold milk, hustled Christmas trees; I sold candles during the Blackout. It was important for me to really knowand understand my feelings about living before I entered that unbelievable world of Ballet or whatever. Dancers who don't really live can never add that life, that something extra, which takes the choreography beyond entertainment and makes it something more, makes it art."

The exploration into different areas of life and dance brought Sallid to upstate New York to choreograph a show for migrant workers. Then on to the New York Shakespeare Festival,where he choreographed Edgar White's play, *Les Femmes Noires*, for Novella Nelson, and later, a T.V. special with Jose Feliciano and Peggy Flemming.

It is this variety of experiences that has enabled Sallid to think in terms of concept and creation. The numerous activities have also given him the experience and the confidence to venture out and put something together of his own. "If I had gone straight into a ballet company I'd have no idea of what a 35mm camera is about, or about directing or organizing an establishment."

The establishment Sallid refers to is Place and Visions Dance Studio. The studio is a multi-faceted center which teaches dance, showcases talent, rents space to various groups, and, finally houses *The New Art Ensemble*. Both the studio and the company are Sallid's children. He has, in a sense, given birth to them and provided the necessary energy, love and money which keeps the two alive.

The dancers of *The New Art Ensemble*—Shirley Brown, Dyane Harvey, Ann Marie Spector, John Parks, Kamal Abdula and Ronald Dunham—are all special to Sallid because they are fantastic technicians on the dance floor, and they, says Otis, "are really good people."

The dancers, in turn, like working with Sallid because, "He's a genius, he's just fabulous," says Shirley Brown. Dyane Harvey enjoys the artistic liberties in Otis' work. "I'm very free to makedecisions about how I want movement to feel. Other choreographers have planned exactly how you should feel when doing their work. It makes you feel like a puppet."

Sallid understands that two energies are better than one so he sees dancers as actors that should be given the space to add flesh and bone to the choreography and to bring to the work their individual insights. Sats Sallid, "I really get off on the marriage."

Combining dance with other medium furthers Sallid's attempt to create and add new dimensions to dance. The young choreographer wants to incorporate film with dance, to give both art forms extra feeling, extra meaning. "It seemscrazy," says Otis, "but I'd like to have a smell in a dance film. Things have their own odor and flavor. Dance studios don't stink but the energy has a definite odor to it. So we should smell that as well as hear and see it, to get that third or fourth dimension."

I'd like to film dance as a director and I'd like to use film in dance. Off the top of my head, I'd love to have this building projected on a wall and people walking in and out. It's a flat dimension· which gives the illusion of strangeness. Its very simulating, but there's so much more because I can take you anywhere with film, to the South Pole and back to Harlem in an instant."

For Sallid, the dance world is an area of exploration and experimentation. It's a plateau from which new life can be given language. Sallid brings to this arena a fresh mind, and the relentless stamina to work until the new form takes shape, and the child is born making the sounds of new life. ✿

ADEMOLA

Cont'd from page 37

inserted, which many people have different opinions on. I call it the universal man, and if you notice, it has the symbol of atomic energy in his head. You'll find that this figure is an underlying element in a great deal of my work. It's a series that I call *PASSAGE THROUGH TIME AND SPACE*. This figure is inserted for the simple reason that I want the people, even though I am taking their minds out into space, into themselves, into their inner consciousness, to have a reflective reference point. And that's what that particular figure is serving as.

I am still probing. That's very important to understand: I'm reaching out, and I'm searching for new forms, because we must find forms that can, in fact, unite Black People into a new order that is on the way. And by new order I mean that there have to be new directions in our struggles for liberation, and nationhood, and a very important part of that struggle is going to depend upon how open and how direct our minds are. It's very important that we have a direction, but at the same time it's very important that our minds are open for new ideas, new thrusts, and that there's a feeling of a universal consciousness, of being in touch with the universe. That should be part of the new thinking towards nationhood.

I stress direction because I don't think that we will ever reach the point where we're just doing art for art's sake. I think that it's imporant that art always have a direction towards something, and in this particular case the Black people can't afford to be directed towards anything but building a nation, building a place in the world for Black people.

The forms that I am now propagating are really new and old simultaneously. I am preparing people for ritual. And I don't want anyone to misunderstand or get spooky about it. "Ritual" simply means a formula or set of formulas and equations that ultimately then do a number of things. They bind things together, they set directions and in general they enhance the knowledge of a people. My art is laying a foundation for future rituals which will begin to unite people. Also, I should hope that it's preparing the mind for some of the future directions that are going to be necessary for our people.

By this I mean that we're going to have to be prepared to be open-minded enough to look at solutions that are going to be offered by our future leaders and which may not necessarily be fully understood by people. I'm trying, hopefully, to instill a kind of faith in our integrity through the work, through the integrity of thinking people. So that we can in fact begin to think as one. That's been one of the problems with Black people; that we ponder and question so much sometimes that we miss the boat. And this is one of the things which I hope that my work will begin to do, to enhance the mind. ✿

Cont'd from page 25 **OSCAR BROWN JR**

Oscar: Well, first of all, I think that you must have a great deal of determination and desire in yourself. There's been numerous people who I've known in my life who apparently had greater talent as singers, as writers, or as performers than I. And then there are others that I know who have gone on into show business but they flagged off, they took "no" for an answer. They were discouraged, sometimes through no fault of their own. Your mother will tell you, "oh son, go and get a job, put down that horn, you're making too much noise and it's disturbing the neighbors." A daddy will tell his daughter, "No, I don't want any daughter of mine in show business!" You can understand that in a way. That will divert people. Sometimes they get themselves in situations in life where they're married or have responsibilities that they can't. . .you have to stick to it! First of all. Then I say, **Be*Excellent**!! Set a standard of excellence for yourself. It takes about as much effort to be excellent as it takes to be mediocre. Sometimes a little less.(laugh) So be excellent. If you get to the point of being a professional, you have a responsibility to your art, to your craft. You have a responsibility to show up prepared to perform and to entertain at the appointed hour when the ticket said so. When the TV went on and it said you're going to be on a show, you should show up and you should show up **well prepared** tp do the best you can at what you are doing.

There is a great deal of reward in that. The problem is the struggle or the fight, but that is what makes it valuable, because it wasn't easy. If a belch was difficult then it would be worth something, but since it isn't it isn't worth anything. Everybody just burps and nobody cares or pays a nickel for it. But if you train yourself to sing, ahh, that's something else, to act, ahh, that's something else. You've put an effect into that thing, you've cultivated your talent. If you get a gift. . .my religion, which is pretty personal. . .if you get a gift, the only way to say thanks for that gift is to cultivate it. If you give me a plant and you come over to my house a month later and the plant is dead, no matter how effusively I thanked you, you know that I didn't appreciate the gift. You give me a dog and you come over and the dog is all mangy and sick. Then you know that I didn't care about that gift. That's the same thing with your talent. If you have a talent for writing, cultivate that thought, man, get down with it, really be good. Look at some other writers, read, study, enhance that. and that way you say thanks

for the gift and you make more of it.

Bob: When you were in England in 1963 performing at the Prince Charles Theatre, the London Times referred to you positively as "a genius." How do you respond to the term or label genius?

Oscar: Well, people are of genius, and genius is a lot of hard work. Genius has to do with the answer to the question before, as far as being excellent is concerned. Now if I were to be put into an automobile shop and asked to fix a car, nobody would ever think that I was a genius. I'm not a genius across the board. If I am a genius, whatever that means, what it means to me is that I worked my ass off to be **good.** ✿

PIRI THOMAS   *Cont'd from page 14*
with the poetry of Lola Rodriquez.

Hector: Is it a dramatic story?

Piri: Yes. I've been working on it for five years. I have been writing even when there were no doors open for me, after *Down These Mean Streets* and *Savior, Savior.* They wanted me to write what they wanted me to write. This was the offer, and I turned it down. I said, I want to write **Savior, Savior Hold My Hand.** "No, it ain't gonna work, it ain't gonna go." When I wrote the first book in prison, I had a corny title picked, like *Home Sweet Harlem.* When I came out, I found out that it had been thrown in the incinerator. It was my only copy, that I had painfully, beautifully and creatively imprinted to pass away the time, to kee from thinking about the parole board. When I found out, I went to the bedroom, and I sat on the edge of the bed, and I said, "Wow," 'cause there were some people already interested in publishing the book and I felt two big, hot tears of anger coming into my eyes. So I said, "Hey, man, cool." I talked to myself. "You wrote it once, you'll write it better." And out of that was born *Down These Mean Streets.* What I'm trying to tell you is, there ain't no such word as defeat, unless it's those you walk on.

Hector: You mentioned earlier that in prison you got close to the Muslim belief. What effect has Islam had on you as a writer?

Piri: The Muslim brothers in prison didn't look as servile as the other men, and they would look, on a peer level, to any guard. And it wasn't arrogant. It was just that there was a dignity to the way they walked. And while I was in prison,   I also delved into Buddhism, Confucianism, Catholicism and Protestantism; and the religions and philosophies. I read the works of Friedrich Nietzche and other philosophers. I have done some heavy reading, Bro, with a big, fat dictionary. (laugh) In

prison, I came to realize that I had to deal with my head, that I had a brain, and that was a power.

Cal: Do you feel that music, and consciousness of the way in which music works, can influence a person's writing?

Piri: To me, music shall always be the soul, and writing, the heartbeat. I am swayed by music, bro. Sometimes I need no music, preferring the sound of silence. But sometimes I need (moves as if playing congas; making conga sounds). Music is the feeling that I get when I'm walking in the street. Or it's a love scene. If you have a film, and it has no music, man, it's really boring,.because when I watch a movie and I see a guy running down the street and then jumping over a fence, and then (makes sounds simulating dramatic movie music), it's incredibly motivating; it inspires and uplifts.

Cal: There has been talk of your doing a musical with Willie Colon.

Piri: I've spoken to Willie Colon, and we still have to discuss and plan the concept behind the work. I don't believe in haste now, because with patience, an elephant can sock if to a flea. The important thing is quality. The musical is called *Sabado Morning,* and a sister named Lydia is capturing the Black essence of what it's all about. Willie Colon will capture the Puerto Rican essence.

Hector: Do you think that there's a difference between the Black essence and the Puerto Rican essence?

Piri: Oh, it's not the difference, my brother. It's the variation of the notes. It's all music, bro. We enhance each other. Contemporary musicians are portraying a sound of the future. The writers, a sound of the future. The poets have always seen the future. They can travel. They're time travellers, bro. I do not believe any ideology to be absolute. As a writer, I must be free to fly, to see all the ideologies, and what is this and what is that. To come as a reporter, to say, hey, this is what I have seen; not for any money, because money is secondary. As a writer, I deal with the principles of dignity and responsibility. All of us have to do that.

Cal: As an artist, what is your goal?

Piri: At one time in my life, when I was born from my mother's womb, a very beautiful kid, they tell me, as soon as I reached the age of awareness, I found that I was only going to be tolerated by the ruling class. Then I found out that, just in order to exist, I first had to survive, and between the two, there was not going to be any opportunity for me to live. I decided that If I was afraid of living, then I would truly die. So I decided not to be afraid of living. ✿

we get as rigid and as tight-assed as anything.

Bob: Yet you see so many people who are rigid.

Melvin: Let me explain this to you now. I ain't responsible for "so many people." I have enough trouble making it to the toilet, myself. You dig what I mean? I don't know. An interesting fact, for example, man, is that I've won awards, and this and that, but you know that no one has ever done one of my songs. Nobody has ever covered a tune that I've written. And I got people sayin' how dynomite they are. Ain't nobody ever sang a tune.

Bob: What do you think are the reasons for that?

Melvin: Well, probably, one is content, the other is the form that they were couched in originally. The third is, I don't have a lot of time to be in the bars sayin', "Hey, look, man, you gotta do such and such. . .do my tune."

Cal: What were you talking about when you said that your album was going to give Gladys Knight competition?

Melvin: I didn't say that.

Cal: Oh. You never said that.

Melvin: No. I don't know who. . .

Cal: . . .Somebody wrote it somewhere.

Melvin: Whoaa, now hold it, don't be no fool! 'Cause somebody wrote something somewhere don't mean that you ask me what did I mean, or did I say it. I didn't.

Bob: Your new novel, the fiction piece, **The True American.**

Melvin: That's my bicentennial offering

Bob: To what?

Melvin: What do you mean, to what? To the bicentennial!

Bob: The celebration of the two hundred years that America did what?

Melvin: Uh-huh, right. That's why you buy the book (laughter).

Bob: Who is the "True American", what is the "True American". What are you saying in **The True American?**

Melvin: No, no, no, no, no, uh ahh. That's why you buy the book (laughter). Now, what I **will** say, and what I'm sure you meant, was (laughter), what is **The True American** about. It's about these two cats who meet up in Hell. And, uhh, who break out and. . .come back to the earth, and what happens to them. One of them, and one of us, and that's what it's about. In many ways, I think I've managed to offend just about everybody, and it's a very funny book, man, very funny. Did you read **Sweetback?**

Bob: Yeah!

Melvin: It's sort of like that, you go with it. If you don't go with it. . .its like jazz, if you ain't in the tempo you could

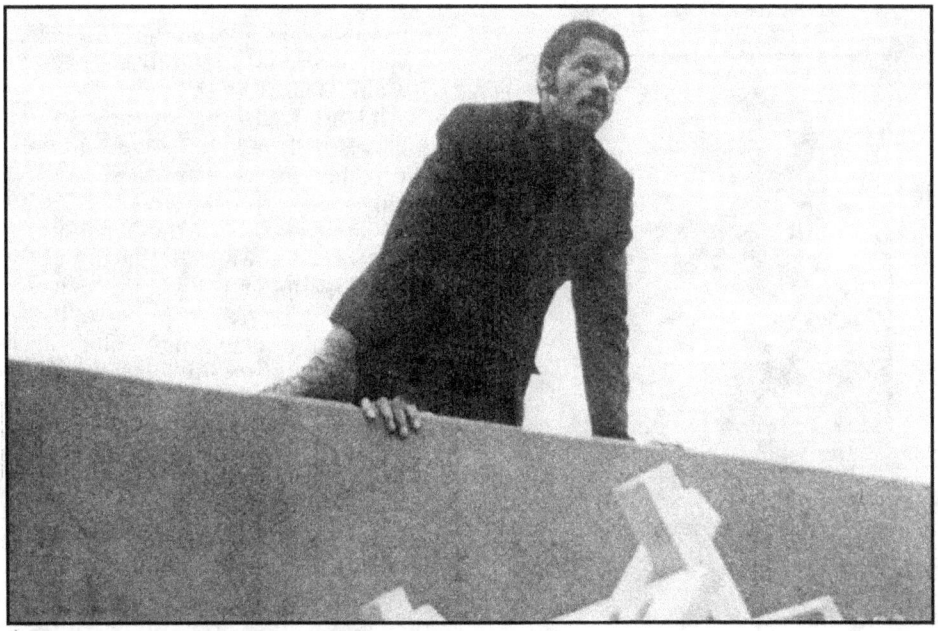

Melvin getting over in *Sweetback.*

EXCERPT FROM "THE TRUE AMERICAN"

Abe scooted down in the back seat.

"O.K., let's go," the Judge said. They drove directly to the Harriman mansion and into the garage.

"Wal, I don't guess nobody saw us, judge," the Sheriff said.

"We ain't through yet," the Judge said. "We gotta get the Prince some clothes."

"What kinda clothes do a Prince wear?" the Sheriff asked.

"I'm sorry, Prince, but we do not have robes...would a suit be all right?" the Judge asked Abe.

The Prince nodded Yes.

"Fine, thank you, Prince...you are very understanding." The Judge sent the Sheriff to the tailor's and ordered the rest of the wardrobe by phone, including several yards of white stuff to make turbans.

Judge Harriman escorted Abe upstairs to a guest room.

"i have a royal house guest this week," the Judge announced to the help. Since the Judge's servants were all Negroes and didn't vote, the Judge used his normal private-life voice. "My guest wants to keep his presence a secret and so do not discuss him with anyone . . .he is one of your people, but of noble ancestry, of course."

The maid who served the dinner was the first to see Abe, and she rushed the news back to the others who were waiting in the kitchen.

"Did'cha see the Prince? the handyman said.

"Is I a Princess? the maid answered.

"Hell, no, ya ain't, the cook said.

"Well I is a Princess, if he is a Prince," the maid said, laughing. "It ain't nothing but a beat-up colored man, with some kinda towel thing wrapped around his head."

"Well, what he doing in there, honey?" the other maid said. "The Judge ain't none too fond of colored folks, as far as I heard tell..."

"What he's doing...is sitting right across from the Judge eating as big as you please, and the Judge ain't batting an eyelash."

"Lordy, Lordy, that's what I call a bold nigger," the handyman said. "Well, more power to him."

All the servants agreed and burst out laughing.

By the next day every Brother and Sister in town had heard the news about the Prince staying up at Judge Harriman's, and everyone was cracking up.

"Lordy, Lordy," they laughed, "if everyone didn't know me in this here count y, I'd buy myself a towel."

All the colored folks went around with a big smile at the joke.

"Sheriff, don't the niggers seem extra happy these days to you?" the deputy asked, looking out the jailhouse window.

These here common old ordinary American niggers that we got around here is always happy. The y is like chillun...come on, play cards. I raise ya seven cents."

After a week of being Judge Harriman's house guest, in the middle of the night and wearing his new wardrobe, Prince Abe was put on the train to Chicago. And for ten years after Prince Abe, no Black man with any common sense ever traveled through the South without carrying a white towel.

55

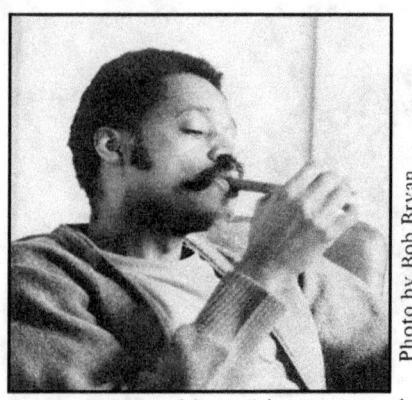

Photo by Bob Bryan

miss the whole thing. It's a story that can be read on a lot of levels. It's sort of like Voltaire or Swift and I know that ain't told you shit, but there's a good way around that: buy the book!

Bob: Are these people, Voltaire and Swift, the people that you. . .

Melvin: Naw. . .its simply the framework, the way the work is framed. It's sort of like **Candide** or **Cullivers Travels**, it's an odyssey. In a way, it could be like Mark Twain.

Bob: Is it autobiographical?

Melvin: Oh, I assume that everything that you write is autobiographical, in that it comes from the quirks of your mind. But the cat starts off at about 1900, the turn of the century: a brother gets put in jail on a humble. He is going to be released the next day, but on another humble he gets sentenced to 3 months on a chain gang. Before that 3 months is up, the nigga that he's shackled to tries to make a break, takes him along and they get caught, and he gets 5 years. Before the 5 years is up he's stacking sand on a levy; he falls over in the water, so he gets life for trying to escape. Before he gets to serve out his life sentence —he's still a very young man— he's killed in an avalanche where he was working in a quarry We're up to about page 5 now, can you dig it (group laughter), and these stones, which are pressed so heavy upon this cat's chest; he takes a breath, and he says, "Jesus Christ", and he's dead. And a voice says, "Yes" and here's this liberal-looking white man sitting behind this desk, floating on this cloud with a pointed beard. "Well, since you know my name" —it's god who's in charge of the admittance into Heaven or Hell, and they ain't got no open admissions (laughs) in heaven. So my man goes to hell. But the devil, trying out a new system, has formed a pit where he doesn't put nothing but Americans, and in this pit niggas get 3 times more rapid advancement. They only have chitterlings and hog maws and so forth and . . .now the white people there are as

miserable as a ___ mutha ; niggas say, "Man, god-dog!" (laugn)

Bob: "This is hell?"

Melvin: Yeah, one of the cats says, "This is hell, man?" They get to ball all the paddy chicks they want to. So the devil defends this; he says, "Look, with such little effort. . .I don't have to use box cars. I don't have to hardly use any torture equipment anymore. I have to use less imps to keep patrolling. . ., 'CAUSE I'm using psychological torture." Since the white folks out-number them 10 to 1, ok, so we got 1/10 that is relatively contented, but these others are so miserable. In fact that's the most successful pit in Hell, the one he's running now, his new experimental modern pit. This is the Hell this cat comes to, and you can go to school in hell. So he goes to school and learns to read and write, 'cause the devil figures that the more you know, the more it hurts. So that's the way it goes.

Bob: Psychological warfare. . .

Melvin: Well, not warfare, but psychological torture.

Bob: Psychological torture, in our lives now. . .especially when I look at the front pages of these newspapers, I'm constantly seeing these kinds of images projected out at us. Even if you don't read it, you've seen these messages, and the ideas start off my day.

Melvin: Hey, exactly; that's exactly right.

Bob: How do we begin to offset the psychological torture and listen to ourselves?

Melvin: Just like we're discussing this book here; you're laughing, or you say, "Hey, man, you know, I see a correlation between this and that." That's the beginning of it all. If we can start fixing it so that we can start

making those correlations, so that we start understanding, that's where it's at. That's what the book is for and the fellow traces, in his search for freedom, the Black political trends that we've followed for years. The first thing he does is, he educate himself very vigorously, so that he can show the white people that black people can really be educated, he bought the hype that white folks laid on him that yall can't be educated;   because if you could we'd open our arms to you: which was the first original Black movement, and that takes us back to Booker T. "We'll form Tuskegee, and then after we've shown that we can be bricklayers and blah blah blah, then they'll take us in." Bullshit!! 'Cause soon as you get that together, they start gerrymandering the place. So then he goes on to the next step, then he goes through communism, then he goes through these various steps, and meantime you're laughing. It's a funny story, and a whole lot of stuff is going on.

Cal: When attempting to put a social-political ideology into artistic terms, how can this be done without becoming didactic?

Melvin: I don't know (laugh) I would sit down and work out the problem. I think in each case I've tried to express a new forms and I've been fairly successful. . .that may take 3 years to say. I don't know! The answer would be what the final product would be. It'd be what I thought when I was faced with the thought of seeing all these mirrored Black people who were mute and never had a voice. I decided that I wanted to give them a voice; I wrote **Ain't Supposed to Die**. That was the entering thesis, to have the wino talk; I wanted to have the hooker talk, I wanted to have the black cop talk. So I gave

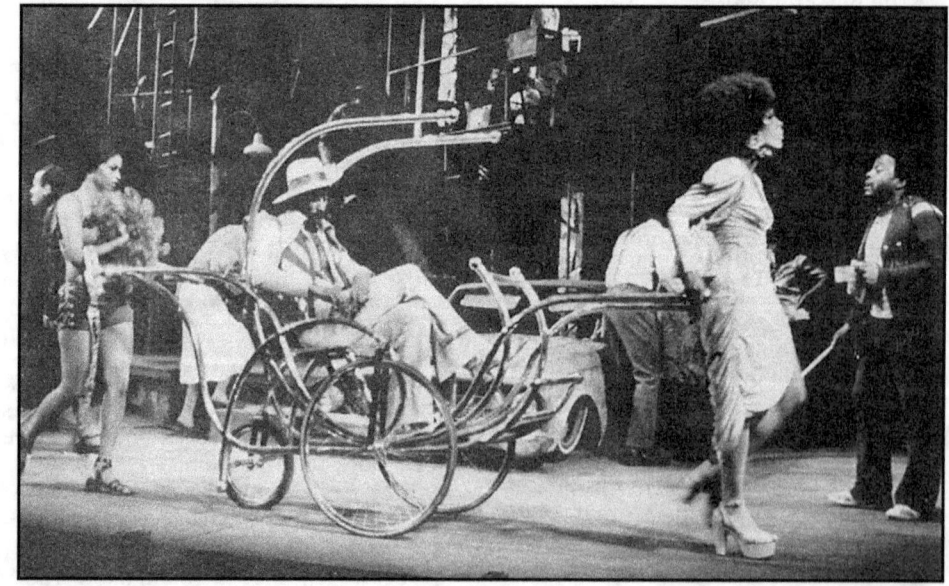

Scene from *Ain't Suppose To Die A Natural Death.*

each one of these people a voice. I didn't arrive at an equation; you don't put the sum, you take the parts and then you add 'em up. That's where the artistry comes, in the doing, that keeps it from being didactic. I could have given a long lecture and stood up on the stage and said, "You must understand we are not a monolith, we are many people", with that point of view. That would have been nice, and it may have been very correct, but it's much hipper to have one guy saying, "Good evening, ladies and gentlemen, preach and praise God, blessings unto the race! Preach and praise God, can you help me to get a little taste." That's one guy; the clerk's saying, "Dee dee dee dee dee, how many drunks in the hall and how come day breaks and don't fall and night falls and don't break and blue eyes ain't satisfied unless his foot's up me." That's a whole 'nother voice, a whole 'nother voice. Or to the disillusioned bar maid: "Love, love, love, yeah, you better believe it." These are different voices. It's better to demonstrate these voices and demonstrate, on top of these voices, the hands on the green ribbons flowing down from the top, who's controlling all of that. That was my solution to that particular problem that I had posed to myself. Just as another project was a different solution to that problem.

Cal: O.K. When you did **Ain't Supposed to Die A Natural Death** you had notes for it, but the actual creation of the play. . .

Melvin: No, no, no, whoaa, slow down. You mean did I have notes for it?

Cal: Yeah, did you have notes for it?

Melvin: There you go, that's better. I had the whole thing written in my mind. I mean I knew what order I wanted it in, I knew where I wanted it to go, and the music was written, this, that and the other. It was there.

Cal: How much did the actors and the. . .

Melvin: They say what the fuck I tell them to say. I'm not limiting myself to the denominator of their vision; that would have been an overall vision.

Gilbert Moses, who directed it. I told him that this is what I wanted done, and how I wanted it done, and he brought his things to it, and that's it. There's a musical structure; I mean, these things were already written.

Bob: So in terms of your technique, do you have a particular kind of technique in terms of your approach to, say, a novel? Do you think it out first, or do you write an outline and then you adhere to the outline?

Melvin: It varies according to each thing. I write one novel one way and I write another novel another.

Bob: How did you write **The True American**?

Melvin: I sat down and I put down 241 pages, and I started to type.

Cal: And filled up the sheets?. . .

Melvin: Uh huh, yeah, and wondered what was going to happen the next day.

Bob: Wait a minute, you had 200 and something sheets and. . .

Melvin: I asked the cat, I said, "How many pages do you want the book to be?" and he said, "About 241 pages," and I took 241 pages and started at one end and stopped at the other.

Bob: Did you know how it was going to end?

Melvin: No idea.

Bob: You mean as you were going through you just. . .

Cal: Were you somehow pacing yourself for 241 pages.?

Melvin: That's how long the man said they were buyin', so that's how long I wrote it.

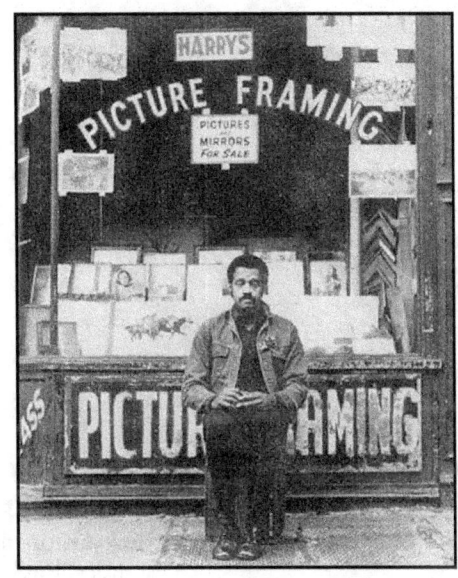

Cal: How do you think it would have turned out if. . .say, for example, if the guy said 300 pages, do you think that it would be different?

Melvin: Probably.

Bob: Do you think that that technique is unusual for a writer?

Melvin: I don't know. I never asked. I never asked nobody. How do I know if its unusual or not? He said 3rd person, 241 pages. . .that's a round length, so I wrote it.

Bob: Did you have a title, did he say . . .did he just want a book from you?

Melvin: Nope. Well, he wanted a Black book, so then the cat got very busy of course. The cat didn't take the book because the book was too hip and they wanted a book about suffering, Black suffering and so forth, and I had gone to ape city on it. I said, OK, and it became a parody of all those things. I said I was going to write 5 pages a day. Then I spent years rewriting it and

honeing it. That's how I did that.

Bob: What was the very first idea that you came out with? The very first thing that you put on paper?

Melvin: The first line.

Bob: Which was. . .

Melvin: I don't know. You want me to look it up?

Bob: Everything sort of just weaves from there.

Melvin: Everything just came from the first line; the second line came just like ABCD. I didn't know what was going to happen the next day. I'd say, "I wonder what's going to happen the next day." I'd wonder what's going to happen tomorrow. It has that quality, that head-on rush.

Cal: When you're writing a novel as opposed to writing a play, or a film-script; do you have to put yourself into a kind of head that this is going to be a novel, or it is it all the same head?

Melvin: It's pretty much the same head, and then after it's done I usually find out what it is. So the head, the whole ambiance is the same. I'm writing a couple of songs now, and they're bubbling around, bubbling, bling bubbling, bling, if I was pushed to it, I guess I could put them on paper today. But I'll put them on paper later on.

Bob: What technique do you use, since you don't know music. . .of putting it down?

Melvin: I numbered all the keys on the piano. I just number them 1-88 and I play 7, 31, 6, 6½; the black keys are the ½ notes.

Bob: And you just give that to an arranger, composer?

Melvin: And I go blink, blink, blink and the cat says, "Oh, you wrote that in so forth and such and such. And that is so forth and such and such." And I say, "Oh, yeah, (laugh) very interesting." But, when I started off, the musicians that I knew at the time, who didn't have any bread at the time; they were too vacuous, man. You say, "Hey, man we going to rehearse at 2, are you gonna help us out?" "Yeah, man. . ." Well, 2 or 3 weeks later, "Well, man, what happened to you?" "Oh, ahh, Jim, my old lady and I got tied up, we had a fight, man and. . ." I got tired of that shit, so I say, well, I'll just do it myself.

Bob: Well, the last question that I have is, if you had to say who Melvin Van Peebles is, who would you say he is?

Melvin: Ahhh, no idea, man. I never . . .I guess a pussyhound.

Bob: Can we quote that?

Melvin: Naw, better not (laugh). I'm just fuckin' with ya (laugh). No , man, you better not say that. I'm low-profilin' it these days! ✿

ALEXANDER
(To NORMAN)
Are you still here? Is J.D. gone?

NORMAN

Yes.

ALEXANDER

Will he be back?

NORMAN

For dinner ... of course.

ALEXANDER

Why are you still here?

NORMAN

I'm leaving in a moment.

ALEXANDER

Hand me that mirror.
(NORMAN passes ALEX a hand mirror)
I done wore this Motherfucker out.
        (HE takes a pill)
Norman ... I'm frightened without you here.
(MUSIC soft coming up. Begin whole MUSIC interlude)
Why are you pretending?
(HE looks at NORMAN, pausing to search his face)
Something's wrong. What is it?

NORMAN
(Quietly, so as not to be overheard)
I've stayed to warn you, Sir.

ALEXANDER

Of what?
        (MUSIC)

NORMAN

You are in mortal danger.

J.D.

(Talking to RITA. Confidential so as not to be overheard)
It was reported in the press today ... that a geologist has discovered in the area of the Asian Sea in the depth of the sand, a pulse. It's reported its tentacles are attached to nothing but the earth itself. They're suspicious as hell about the whole thing. The only logical explanation is that they have discovered the center of life.
        (Pause)
... It is dead still. Nature is dead still. You're to be terminated.
(J.D. and RITA watch ALEX and NORMAN)

NORMAN
I have to leave, Sir.
(NORMAN smiles again. HE starts to move quickly from the room)

ALEXANDER

Norman will you tell me what you're talking about!
*(NORMAN can be seen grabbing his coat and a small duffle bag and running towards the front door.
MUSIC interlude continues.
MUSIC out)*

NORMAN! ... NORMAN! ... NORMAN! ...
*(A door can be heard to slam.
RITA runs into the downstairs room. A dressing gown on. J.D. sits in a corner downstairs looking at them. Listening like a frightened child.
MUSIC interlude stop)*

RITA

What's the matter?

ALEXANDER

Who are these people you have coming tonight?

RITA

Good God, why are you so upset?

ALEXANDER

WHO ARE THEY?

RITA

He produces very important movies and he's rich as hell!

ALEXANDER

WHAT'S THEIR NAMES!

RITA

Philippe ... Philippe DeValois and his wife Jane. Put your jacket on, they'll be here any minute now. Did that son of a bitch leave here without setting out the mixes for the cocktails?

ALEXANDER

You pusillanimous faggot!

RITA

NOW LISTEN HERE! ...

ALEXANDER

Don't you check people out before you accept them!

RITA

THEY'VE GOT MONEY!

ALEXANDER

I'M AN ARTIST ... AND YOU PASSED A DEATH SENTENCE ON ME!

RITA

WE'RE THREE MONTHS BEHIND IN THE MORT—
GAGE, AND THEY'VE THREATENED TO RAISE
OUR RATE, YOU DUMB MOTHERFUCKER!

ALEXANDER

... NATURE IS DEAD!

RITA

Listen, you start that shit at the dinner table and I'll do
something I'm not responsible for!

ALEXANDER

What are you responsible for?

RITA

For keeping food on the table. To running this God-
damn house. Relieving you on Saturday nights like a
human urinal ... For you, pimp!

ALEXANDER

What?

RITA

PIMP!

ALEXANDER

WHORE!

RITA

PIMP!

ALEXANDER

WHORE!

RITA

PIMP! Baby wants her fantasy! I want it. Now, put your
dinner jacket on and wear cologne. When they leave
here we will have something, if I have to steal their
wallets. Wash everywhere ... you never know how far
they expect you to go.

ALEXANDER

PHILIPPE DE VALOIS IS SATAN! ... YOU'VE IN—
VITED HIM HERE!

RITA

He's rich. And White! And he's the devil! And you're a
Nigga. This will have to be a revolution of wits. So far
you're just one of the play people. Don't try and get real
tonight.

ALEXANDER

What?

RITA

You must learn to appreciate the better things hell has
to offer.

ALEXANDER

SATAN IS NOT GOD!

RITA

In hell he is ... this is Nigga hell ... Get dressed!
(RITA leaves the room.
J.D. leaves after her.
J.D.'s film starts. ALEX speaks over it.
MUSIC)

ALEXANDER

Some
new leaf
that has come to fore
in my head.
Some
increase of appetite
Some Unleavened bread.
Some decayed bone
through which my
blood
has fled.
Some obedience
to history
is dead.
To unlearn the
great white idea.
To back it through
'my
core.
This sermon that entered through my ear
yet stimulates
no more.
Some piece of European truth
that has dearly come apart
emaciates my blood
and manipulates
my heart.
I have come to understand
through the accident of stress
that art devoid of me is
genocide,
at best.

(we hear laughter coming from the dining room. The
lights come up in the dining room. RITA sits at the
head of the talbe. ALEXANDER's chair at the foot is
empty. J.D. sits eating. Sitting at either side of RITA
are PHILIPPE and JANE. THEY are both attractive
tall blonds. THEY are in their thirties. ALL are in
evening clothes. PHILIPPE lights the candles on the
table with his lighter. EVERYONE seems very jolly,
dinner is finished. THEY are caught in conversation
as THEY glance at a film being run on a big screen
above them. The film, a slow-motion film of hun-
dreds of naked men, Black and White, being herded
by armed guards. Film continues over party till it
finishes. A gentle jazz samba now and then)❀

Inquiries concerning Black Picture Show should be
made to Reed, Cannon and Johnson at 2140 Shattuck
Avenue, Room 311, Berkeley, California, 94704. For
mail order, send $2.95 plus $0.26 mailing cost.

were so in tune. . .You figure maybe once in a while you hear a little kid who sings so much in tune, but here was these little kids, all daughters. It was a real trip for my head, and I realized where I was coming from, where all these things were coming from. What happened is that all of these influences became one with me. That's why you can hear classical in my music; you can hear Rock, you can hear Jazz in it, but you can't say, well, that section there was classical and that was Jazz.

Bob: You synthesize.

Jon: It's everything. You hear it all as you go. It's like a rainbow. Many people think it's new music but the music has been around here before all of us. I am not doing anyting new. The music is not new, music is old as. . .

Bob: It's how you put it togehter. . .

Jon: It's what I'm expressing as an individual artist. This is what's coming. I can't write a poem like Felipe Luciano, because that is his feeling y'know, but I can understand it.

Bob: You were taking voice lessions with Professor Boatner, weren't you?

Jon: YESSSS. . .that is the master. I pray that he live forever because I don't want to go to anyone else. If he should ever pass I would just have to remember everything he has taught me and just maintain it without having to go to him. When you go to your teacher he can always tell you something that you think is right but that you weren't doing. No matter how many years you study, there is always something that you can dis-

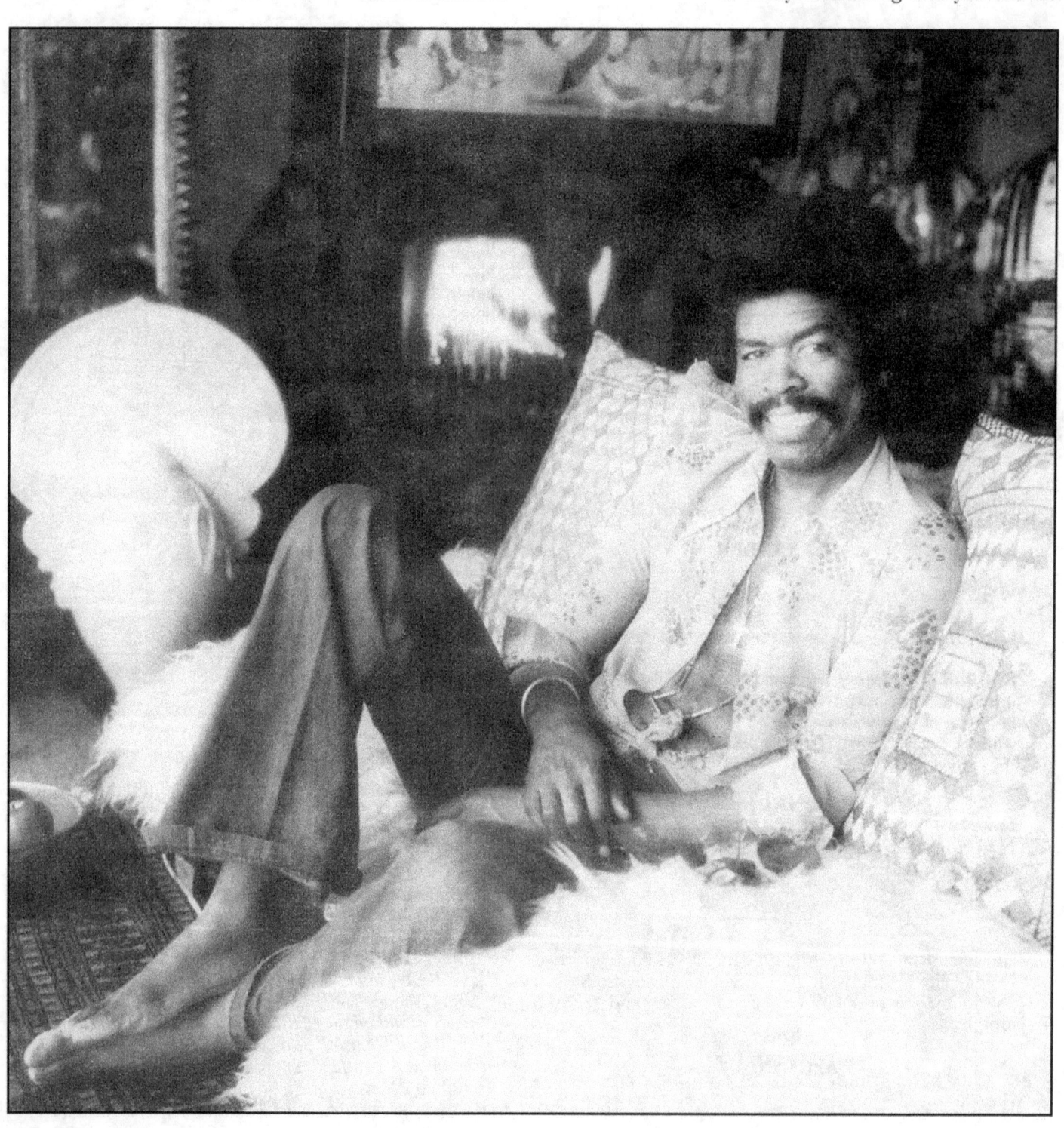

cover. To me he is it! I would never go to nobody else as long as this man is alive.

Bob: Have you developed a particular method of breathing?

Jon: Well, Mr. Boatner showed me how to use my diaphragm very well, but he's mad at me because I don't do it like I should. But sometimes I amaze myself (laughter).

David: When you're chanting, do you use the diaphragm?

Jon: Yes, the chanting does that because I can take a deep breathe (chanting) and you'll stop twice and I'll still be chanting. . .Y'know once you're going to hear it, you're going to hear it, and it's stated that within a seven-year period after you've been touched by Nam Myoho Renge Kyo some way along that period you're going to start to chant. It's all cause and effect. It's like, once you realize the universe inside you, . . .that there are rivers in there, mountains in there; there's everything in there, just like out here, it just looks different. But it's the same principle. When you see a car it has an engine, which is just like a heart so that when the heart is going everything else is going. Everytime they build a computer, it's based upon you.

Cal Wilson: Has living in different places, like New York, affected your writing and how you've conceptualized the music?

Jon: It's affected my music. It really made my music develop from. . .being in NEW YORK alone, with the competition, ahhhh, with the competition. Now I don't know anything else to do, all I do is music, y'know. I said, well, this is my way of living, this is how I'm going to do it, so I better get on the case.

Bob: To the maximum.

Jon: I have to be the best at what I do. I don't want to be better than anyone else. I just want to be the best of what I am.

David: When you started your career, did you have a plan? I'm referring also to the chanting.

Jon: All the chanting does is open you up. It opens up your knowledge and your understanding, your relationship to people. . .like sometimes, now, I can look at someone and get like a connection. It happened twice to me in the last two days. Two different brothers: something about them gave me the feeling that they were in school, but they weren't in school, they were just getting ready to enter. So I saw that. I never thought about a plan. I just wanted to do the music and get better and try to make it. As I get older I see all the different problems that we have to deal with in life, and I realize that by making a lot of money you can change certain things. You can change certain conditions, be-

cause money allows you to change the conditions. Money does not enlighten you, but it will allow me, and maybe some other brothers with the same concern as myself, to buy some schools and get some buildings, and renovate them, and give the neighborhood people a chance to work on these buildings and

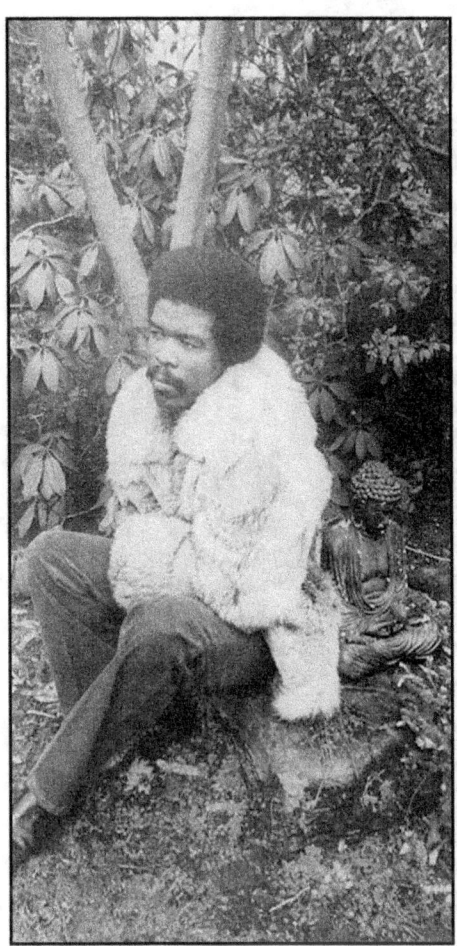

live in them for a decent price; and we don't think about making a million dollars at the end of the year. Just let the mortgage pay itself off, no matter how long it takes. When it's paid off, you develop sanitation facilities in between those developments. The people are concerned about themselves: they have their own schools where their kids can go and they can relate to their blackness and they can also relate to what is wrong with the other.

Bob: How would you describe the people who have gravitated to your music and your concerts?

Jon: What makes me so pleased about the people who attend a Jon Lucien concert is that all of them are spiritually involved. They all are. My agent says, "Jon, I've never seen an audience like yours. They have a certain age about them, and even if they're young, they have a dignity, a pride, and they are well-dressed even if they're wearing jeans or not. These are respectful people!" He says, "Jon, I don't see these kind of people, where are they

coming from?" I said, do you know something, there are a lot of people who want to be what they are, but because of the way our society is, they remain to themselves and they stay to themselves. But when they see somebody out there like myself or James Brown, they usually look at us and say "Oh, wow—yeah we got somebody out there," and they get behind you, and they come out, man. It's like, someone once told me, "People who like your music, they like the better things in life," and I said, well, anybody likes the better things in life. The person told me this to my face, and I couldn't believe this man, and suddenly he was telling me that I am not going to live anymore by my music because I got to do the street sound. I said, tell me something, if you like fine leather, are you going to buy pigskin because you want to wear leather, or are you going to wait until you can buy leather? Tell me! He didn't have no answer. That's the way it is! There is one thing that I don't want my audience to get carried away with and that is forgetting that I am a human being, just like them.

David: 'Cause it's the same trip. As far as your music goes, are you going to let yourself become commercialized?

Jon: The funny thing about commercialism is, when something gets over, that's what "commercial" is.

David: It's just a term.

Jon: Yeah. . .When I record, I don't want to make every album to be like the RASHIDA album (laugh). I am a young man, 34 years old, hoping to live for as long as I can, and in each step in my life, I want to see an accomplishment. I want to see a growth, and the moment I make an album that doesn't go beyond the last one I did, I'm going to hang it up. It's all over.

David: A lot of people that I speak with have equated your kind of singing (there I go with the categories again) with that of Johnny Mathis. You know, "the new Johnny Mathis." How do you react to that?

Jon: I'm flattered, because Johnny Mathis is a master. He is a master vocalist, without a doubt, and as a matter of fact I tried to sing like him at one time. But my strongest influences came from Nat Cole and Jesse Beldon. He's the brother who wrote EARTH ANGEL. He had made two albums for RCA, and he died in a car accident. He made one called JUST JESSE BELDON, and one called MR. EASY. He had the same kind of velvet texture like Nat King Cole, but it was "earth." Whereas Cole was very sophisticated, "Dance Ballerina Dance", this guy Beldon was, "Another Bride, Another Groom". But he was that velvet-funky.

David: How did you get exposed to him?

Jon: Well, I was exposed to his record at a radio station in St. Thomas. I saw his face on an album that was laying around there, and there was a look on this man's face that told me that there was something happening here. I took

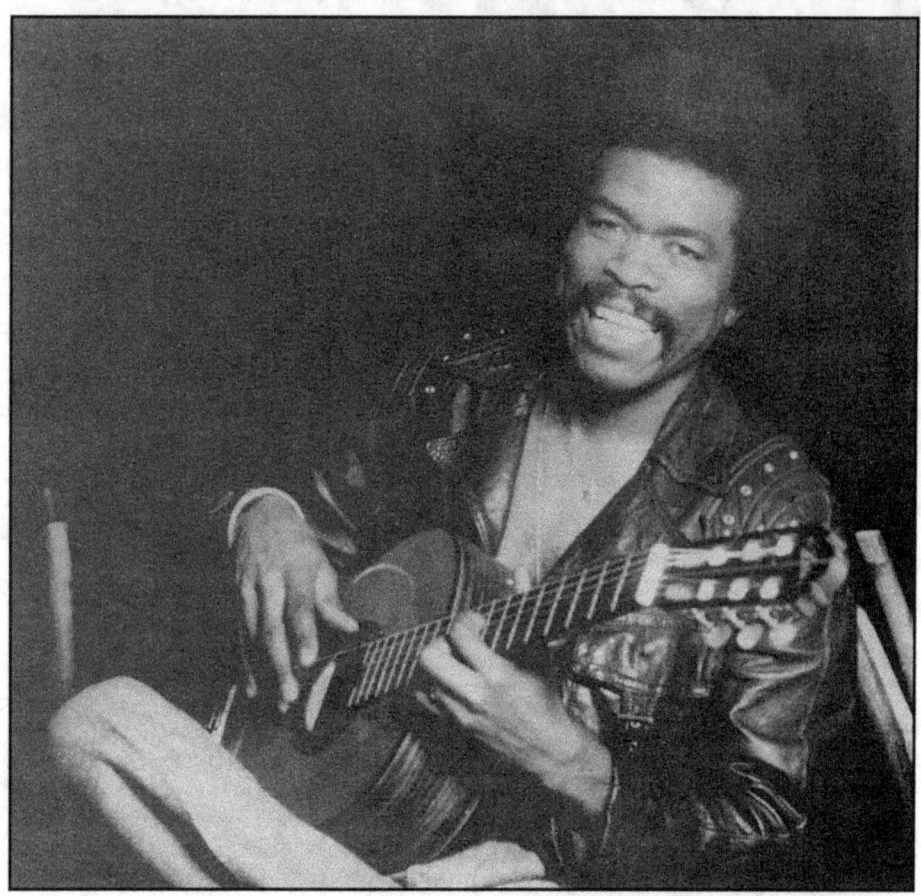

his album home, and this guy sang *My funny Valentine* . I said, "Whatttttt" (laugh) and I used to sit down daily and try to sing like this man.

David: How old were you then?

Jon: I must have been 17 or 18, and here I was an island boy who could hardly talk, but I was trying to get it, like this guy (laugh). And later on I discovered that, hey, you are not going to be cool unless you have your own identity, so you had better start to look for it, and that's when I got really deep into people like John Coltrane and Miles Davis. I really listened to their horns. I don't sing like their horns, but their horns gave me direction. I use words to sound like a cello. So you may notice that I go (makes a cello sound); I love that cello sound. The voice is one of the most fantastic instruments there is; the voice could be a drum or anything. You must apply it, and most vocalists don't apply their voices in most instances. So that's another reason why they look at me, because my African heritage is very profound. The rhythmic life of my heritage, my attitude; I am very Black. I have no objections whatsoever to the fact that I am who I am. I am me and this is what I am. Take it or leave it. I have a gift, and I am not going to let anybody strangle it. Whatever supreme power brought me here to communicate, that's what I'm going to do.

David: Going back to RASHIDA, I notice that ¾ of the people at your concerts have been women, and. . .

Jon: You see, they're not in love with me, maybe they love what I'm saying.

Bob: Because they've waited so long to hear it?

Jon: Yes, this is how I look at it. It's like they're saying, "At last somebody has come by that's saying something that's making some sense." Don't call me THE PROPHET OF LOVE. I ain't no prophet of love, and I think that anybody that allows himself to be called a prophet of love is just as full of it as the people who are calling him that. But I don't want the ladies to think that I'm funny either. I'm not a faggot by any means. But I don't want them to think that I can satisfy them all. I'm just happy to know that they appreciate me and I can get my records to be sold and I can keep on singing. . .and I love women, y'know, without a doubt. But I know there are brothers like me, and the brother don't want to express himself like I'm doing, but I can get away with it

and be honest, because it's music. And hopefully by being honest I can inspire somebody else to bring out their honesty and just be what they really feel with themselves. I don't want to think about, "Hit me, get down" and all that kind of stuff. What am I doing for your mind? Nothing! But if I can say something that makes you say, "Y'know, I thought about that". . .'Cause you just can't go around talking to people like this. You just have to be yourself, and it will just come into being. There's always somebody whom you can associate with. You don't have to have the universe to yourself. I cannot please everybody, so If somebody says "I don't like him", well, hey, there it is, 'cause I know that I don't like everybody I hear. I don't like everybody, but I like some.

Bob: In some of today's song-writing there seems to be a strange interpretation of the male-female relationship.

Jon: Yeah, yeah. Your mother is a woman, and if you can't speak with decency to a woman. . .and if you don't realize it by now, the woman is the strongest and most powerful being down here. Man, she carries a human inside her for nine months, like the flowers; they both give fruits. This is exactly what the woman is doing. I may not fulfill her every desire by being her one and only love. But whatever I share with her, like I hope that she realizes that this is real and genuine. First of all I would love to tell women to exercise her intelligence, and speak up, "Let's communicate," because she's not this table or this saucer that I put the cup in to drink my tea. She's another human being. So that you have to treat her like one.

Bob: What period of your life are you in now, Jon?

Jon: Probably the most difficult, right now. It's hard to describe the elements and what they do to you. I'm sure you know what I mean. . .with these obstacles. I mean, you see that you're making an achievement, and at the same time you're seeing all these obstacles. But that is the test of your faith, and I think that I'm going through the biggest test right now. I don't know how to describe it to you. In my daily life, there are certain emotions that come on me. Now that I'm getting a little bit more recognized in the business, the pressures are getting heavier with the people

Bob: What is success to you, Jon?

Jon: Success to me is when I arrive at the point where I'm comfortable and I can help other people to be just as comfortable as me. The only way that I can do that is by achieving my goals. Success to me is to help somebody else develop, and seeing that they get over because of my help. ✿

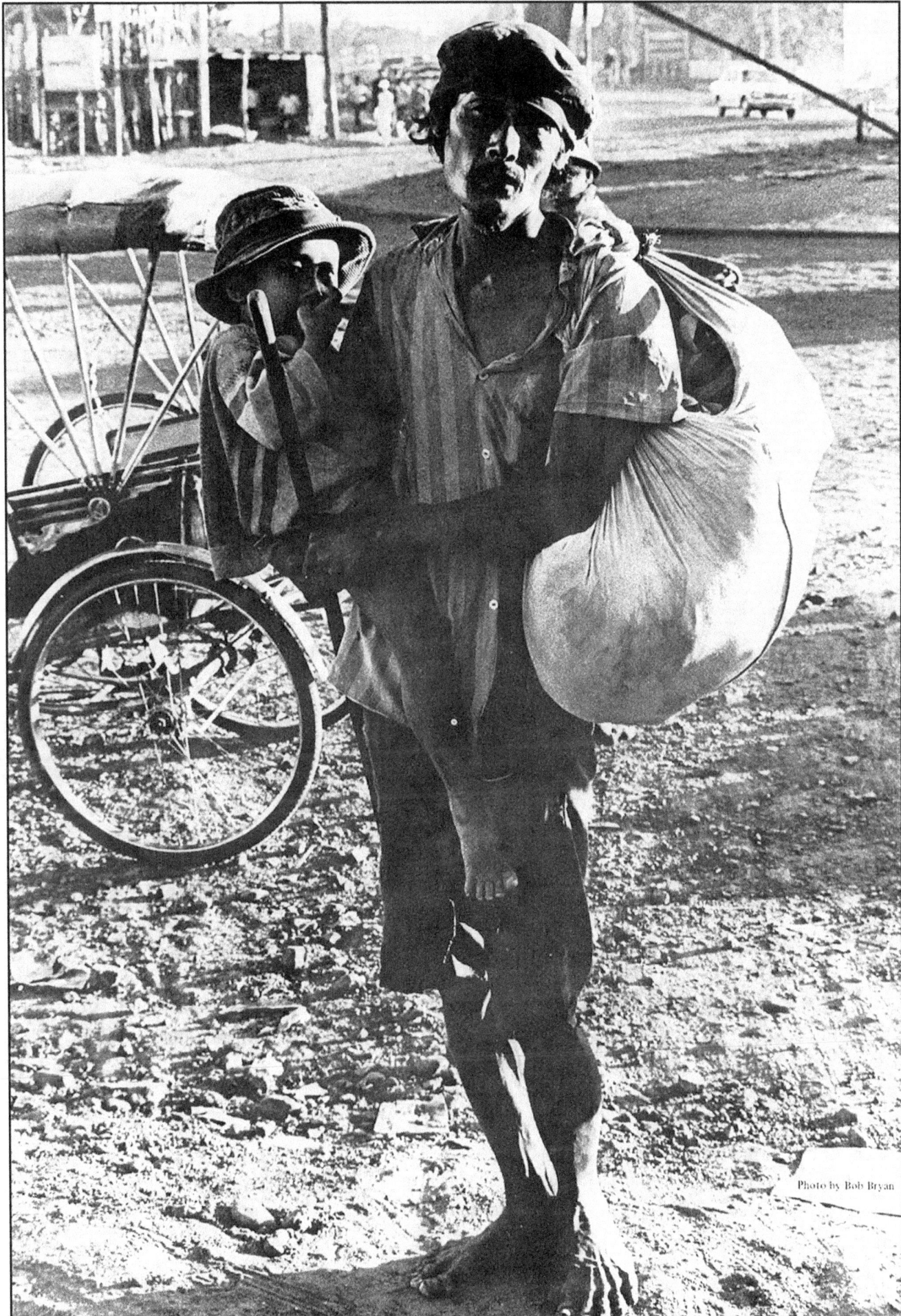

Photo by Bob Bryan

PUBLISHER ACKNOWLEDGEMENTS

The rebirth of the Special 1974 Commemorative Reissue Series of IMPRESSIONS Magazine of the Arts is a special labor of Love for us. 1974 witnessed an explosion of powerful & creative expressions in: Theater Arts, Poetry, Art, Music, Photography, Literature, Dance / Choreography, Theater Review, Film, Critique, Nutritional Advice & Fashion.

As the independent Publisher of IMPRESSIONS MAGAZINE OF THE ARTS I am very proud to be able to again re-introduce to this new generation, the power and fertile imagination of these generous and talented contributing artists and creators, who worked so hard to honestly represent themselves and their people during this tumultuous, passionate and exciting period.
IMPRESSIONS MAGAZINE is truly a historical and educational snapshot of the times.

MELVIN VAN PEEBLES	CALVIN WILSON
JON LUCIEN	HECTOR LINO, JR.
OSCAR BROWN, JR.	ROBERT BRYAN
BARBARA ANN TEER	JOYCE DUKES
BILL GUNN	DAVID EDWARDS
CLEAVON LITTLE	JANN PARKER
DICK ANTHONY WILLIAMS	VICTOR MANUEL ROSA
PIRI THOMAS	NTOZAKE SHANGE
OTIS SALLID	JOHN A. WILLIAMS
DR. ADEMOLA	ERNELL ELIZABETH WORRELL
ADRIENNE KENNEDY	MACHITO
THE NATIONAL BLACK THEATER	NAOMI SIMMS
WOODIE KING, JR.	THE SPINNERS
LEROY CLARKE	IMPACT
CAROLINE ANDERSON	MICHAEL JAMISON
BRENT JENNINGS	CECIL TAYLOR
SONIA MANZANO	PAT GLENN

GV SERIES IMPRESSIONS Magazine of the Arts Publications

GV16 **IMPRESSIONS Magazine of the Arts (December 1974)** -Reissue Date 07/29/2012
GV17 **IMPRESSIONS Magazine of the Arts (Spring 1975)** - Reissue Date 08/15/2012
GV18 **IMPRESSIONS Magazine of the Arts (October 1975)** - Reissue Date 08/19/2012
GV19 **IMPRESSIONS Magazine of the Arts (June 1976)** - Reissue Date 08/27/2012

With much love & respect, I sincerely thank you from the top of my heart.

Robert Bob Bryan, Founder / Publisher
Loida Bryan, Co-Executive Producer
website: http://www.graffitiverite.com
e-mail: bryworld@aol.com

www.ingramcontent.com/pod-product-compliance
Lightning Source LLC
Chambersburg PA
CBHW081241180526

45171CB00005B/506

* 9 7 8 1 4 7 9 1 7 8 4 7 6 *